W. H. G. Kingston

The Seven Champions of Christendom

W. H. G. Kingston

The Seven Champions of Christendom

ISBN/EAN: 9783337172442

Printed in Europe, USA, Canada, Australia, Japan

Cover: Foto ©Lupo / pixelio.de

More available books at **www.hansebooks.com**

THE

SEVEN CHAMPIONS

OF

CHRISTENDOM

By

W. H. G. KINGSTON

Glasgow: GOWANS & GRAY, LTD.

London: R. BRIMLEY JOHNSON

1904

THE present is an exact reprint of the first edition, of which the title-page is given below, a few obvious misprints having been corrected.

The Seven Champions of   Christendom   A New Version   from the most ancient chronicles and records, and   all other authentic and reliable   sources of information   especially adapted for the enlightenment, edification, and   instruction of the rising generation By William H. G. Kingston.   Author of " Ernest Bracebridge," etc.   London :   Sampson Low, Son, and Co.   47, Ludgate Hill.   1861.

PREFACE

THE following pages should not go forth into the world without due acknowledgment being made to that worthy old Dominie, Richard Johnson, to whose erudite but somewhat unreadable work the author is so largely indebted. As he flourished at the end of the sixteenth century, and the commencement of the seventeenth, great allowances should be made for his style, which is certainly not suited to the taste of this generation. It is to be hoped that the present version, while much of his vivid imagery is retained, may be free from his more glaring errors. And, thus quoting the Dominie's dedication :—

"TO ALL COURTEOUS READERS

THE AUTHOR

WISHETH ENCREASE OF VERTUOUS KNOWLEDGE.

"Gentle readers, in kindness accept my labours, and be not like the chattering cranes, nor Momus' mates, that carp at everything. What the simple say I care not ; what the spightful speak I pass not ; only the censure of the conceited I stand unto ; that is the mark I aym at ; whose good likings if I obtain, I have won my race ; if not, I faint in the first attempt, and so lose the quiet of my happy goal.

"Yours in kindness and command,

"R. J."

CONTENTS

CONTENTS

THE SEVEN CHAMPIONS OF

CHRISTENDOM

CHAPTER I

Who has not heard of the Seven Champions of Christendom—of the wonderful adventures they went through—of the dangers they encountered, and the heroic deeds they performed? Should any persons exist ignorant of the history of those noble knights, let them with attentive ears now listen to my veracious chronicle.

Gallant and dauntless as were all those seven heroes, yet not one equalled in valour " St. George of Merrie England." Many countries have in consequence claimed him as their own especial Champion. Portugal, Germany, Greece, and Russia, for what is known to the contrary, would be glad to have him ; but we have proof undoubted that to England he alone belongs, even if we did not see him, on many a golden guinea, engaged in his desperate encounter with the most terribly terrific and greenest of green dragons. Not only are his orders worn by nobles, but by British monarchs themselves, while, in memory of his heroic deeds, they lead forth their armies under his banner. However, many long years have passed away since he astonished the world by his prowess. Of royal birth was his mother, the daughter of one of

England's early kings ; a Duke and High Steward of the realm was his father. Of the name of the king history is most mysteriously silent, or of the extent of his dominions ; but there can be no doubt that the ancient city of Coventry was situated within them, and that, if not the principal, it was one of the principal cities of the realm, and, moreover, that a prison existed there on the silent system. Thus, when people are unfit to be spoken to, it is said, by a figure of speech, that they are sent to Coventry.

In Coventry the Lord High Steward and his royal bride resided. Now, some time before the Princess was about to present her husband with a babe, she dreamed a dream ; it was enough to terrify her, for she dreamed that, instead of a smiling infant, she should have to nurse a little green dragon. To nurse a small crocodile or alligator, or even a young hippopotamus, would have been bad enough, but a green dragon, with claws and a long wriggling fork-pointed tail, was out of the question ; the very idea was enough to drive her distracted. The Lord High Steward was a man who always took the bull by the horns in a dilemma, and so he resolved forthwith to take steps to solve the mystery. He had heard that in the Black Forest in Germany there lived a powerful enchantress, Kalyb by name, who would, without doubt, be able at once to give him all the information he required. Sir Albert, for that was the High Steward's name, instantly set off across the seas, accompanied only by his faithful Squire, De Fistycuff. They bore offerings of gold and silver and precious stones with which to propitiate her.

For many days they voyaged, tossed by the stormy billows, and for many days they travelled on till they arrived at the dreary precincts of the Black Forest. Boldly plunging into it, they reached a dense part of the wood, composed of withered, hollow, and distorted trees, whence proceeded sounds the most unearthly and terrific. The dismal croaking of the night raven, the hissing of serpents, the hoarse bellowing of wild bulls, the roaring of lions, the laughing of hyenas, and other hideous cries of all sorts of savage beasts. Some men would have stood astounded. Not so Sir Albert and his faithful Squire. On they went till they found themselves in front of a dark and lofty rock, within which was seen a vast and gloomy cavern. The entrance was secured by a massive iron gate studded over with huge knots and bars of steel. Near it hung a brazen trumpet, the use of which the Knight full readily guessed. He blew a blast which rung through the vaulted cave, echoing away till the sounds were lost in the distance, while it made the very earth rock and tremble. Scarcely had the echoes of the magic horn died away than a terrifically loud, discordant, hollow voice, proceeding out of the very depths of the cavern, inquired:— "Mortal, what want you here?" Sir Albert briefly told his errand, and said that he had brought gifts which he desired to offer to the famous Enchantress Kalyb, the lady of the Black Forest. As he was a courteous knight, and had spoken the Enchantress fair, so he expected a courteous and satisfactory reply. What, then, was his amazement when he heard these words proceeding from the cavern:—

" Whatever must be—must be there's no doubt;
You've got an answer, and so turn about ! "

In vain he protested that such a reply was far
from satisfactory; that he should go back as wise
as he came ; that it would have been better had he
stayed at home ; that he should have had all his
pains for nothing.   No other answer could he get.
Though a courteous knight, he was yet somewhat
irascible; and this was an occasion to try the temper
of a milder man than a knight of those days.   He
seized the trumpet, and blew till it refused to give
forth any further sound.   He handed it to De
Fistycuff, and told him to blow till he cracked his
own cheeks or the trumpet.   In vain the Squire
puffed and puffed, not a sound could he produce.
He holloed and shouted, and so did De Fistycuff;
but to their united voices no answer was returned.
Then Sir Albert began to shower abuse on the
Enchantress; he told her some awkward truths, and
called her some names which were far from com-
plimentary ; but the only answer he received was in
shouts of hollow and mocking laughter which
proceeded out of the recesses of the cavern.

At length Sir Albert turned his horse's head, and
in high dudgeon rode off, followed by De Fistycuff,
who first pocketed the gifts they had brought to
propitiate the Enchantress.   Dull and dreary was
their homeward journey; and, if truth must be told,
the Lord High Steward could not help feeling
remarkably small at the result of their expedition.
After having been tossed about for many days by a
storm, and made very sick in the German Ocean,
they at length reached Coventry.   The master of
his household, his family physician, and a numerous

assemblage of knights and ladies, rushed out of his castle to tell Sir Albert the news. Neither an hippopotamus nor an alligator had been born to him, but a right merry, rosy, bouncing infant. Alas! however, there was grief in store for the gallant knight, the partner of his joys and cares, his beautiful princess, was dead! Deeply he mourned his loss, and then he inquired if any one could solve the mystery of the dream which had caused him so long a journey. He found that had he waited patiently at home, like a wise man, all would have been known. The smiling infant was brought to him; and then, wonderful to relate, he discovered on its breast the portrait of a green dragon, just as his wife had described it to him; and, moreover, a blood-red cross marked on the boy's right hand, and a golden garter below his knee on the left. "He'll do something wonderful!" exclaimed the proud father; and he was not mistaken.

The name of George was given to the boy; and forthwith the Lord High Steward, retiring from the cares of state, bestowed on him all his thoughts and attention. He selected three nurses to watch over him, called Prudence, Firmness, and Gentleness. One to prepare his nourishment, another to feed him, and the last to lull him to sleep. All would have gone well, but unhappily the boy's grandfather suggested that another nurse was necessary, and Carelessness was introduced into the household.

It should be known that all this time the wicked Enchantress Kalyb had been well aware who it was who had come to her cavern and blown so furiously on her magic horn. Every word the Knight had uttered, and every opprobrious epithet which he had

so lavishly bestowed, had been heard by her. She
nourished, in consequence, in her evil heart, a
spirit of revenge, which she waited a convenient
opportunity to gratify. Oh, anger! oh, loss of
temper! how blind art thou! How dost thou
make wise men become like the most foolish!
Revenge, too, how dost thou, malignant spirit, fall
into the trap thou hast thyself laid, as will be soon
seen!

Wicked Kalyb waited her time. She knew of
the young Prince's birth, she knew how his father
doated on him, and she resolved to carry him off;
but when she heard of the three nurses appointed to
guard over him she despaired of succeeding in her
object. The boy grew and flourished. Every day
he became more beautiful, every day he gave proofs
of a noble and gallant spirit. Truly was he his
father's pride; worthy was he of the admiration of
all the people of Coventry. When, however, Kalyb
found out that Carelessness had become his nurse,
instantly she hurried to the sea-shore; when,
embarking in an egg-shell,—the shell, be it known,
of a huge roc's egg—she set sail for the shores of
England. Quickly she spun over the ocean, round
and round, faster than any ordinary ship could sail,
till she reached the land; and, arriving in the
neighbourhood of Coventry, she hid herself in a
thick wood, till she could pounce out on the young
Prince and carry him off.

However, she had long to wait. Sometimes
Prudence walked out with him, sometimes Gentleness, and sometimes Firmness; and all kept so
careful a watch over him that she had no opportunity of effecting her purpose. At length,

Carelessness one fatal day had charge of him. Kalyb immediately changed herself into a lovely butterfly. Off ran the boy with his velvet cap to catch the fluttering insect. Carelessness sat down on a bank and fell asleep. Soon Kalyb led the boy into the recesses of the forest; then seizing him, in spite of his cries, she placed him in a chariot with ten fiery steeds which she had conjured up, and darting off like a flash of lightning, reached the coast, embarked in her egg-shell, which whirled round and round as before, and then she travelled on till she arrived once more, with her captive, at the magic cavern in the Black Forest. The massive gates flew asunder at a touch of her silver wand, and the Prince found himself among wonders which his imagination had never before conceived, which far surpassed anything he had ever beheld even in the beautiful city of Coventry. He soon, however, grew weary of them, and longed to return to his fond father and careful nurses; but he found himself a prisoner, and no outlet could he discover by which he could make his escape from the cavern—the massive gates prevented all egress to any who had once entered within them.

The wicked Kalyb watched the sorrow of the boy, and knowing that his father was still more sorrowful, rejoiced in her revenge. She had numerous attendants to do her will. Among them was a dwarf, a misshapen, ill-favoured creature. To his care the boy was confided, with directions to beat and teaze him whenever he had nothing else to do. The noble child bore every indignity with equanimity and good humour, and, instead of harbouring revenge, took every opportunity of doing a

kindness to the poor dwarf, who was himself the
peculiar object of the wicked Kalyb's ill-treatment.
Crumpleback was the dwarf's name. Often poor
Crumpleback's body was black and blue with the
pommelling he received from the furious Kalyb,
while his cheeks were thin and haggard from want
of food and rest. One day Kalyb was absent when
Crumpleback addressed the Prince: — "Know,"
said he, "kind boy, that I am a fairy in disguise,
and though less powerful than the fell Enchantress
Kalyb, I may yet circumvent her acts. Your kindness and gentleness, and forgiveness of the injuries I
was forced to do you, have won my heart. I have
vowed to serve you to the best of my power. Let
not Kalyb know what has passed between us, but
wait patiently, and see what will happen." The
young Prince thanked the fairy, and his hopes of
escaping once more revived. He had long to wait.
In the mean time, whenever Kalyb was absent, the
seeming dwarf gave him instructions in all the arts
which would fit him to become an accomplished
knight. Book learning, though not much in vogue
in those days, was not neglected. Sometimes the
fairy put a shining sword into his grasp, and
showed him how to wield it with a force no one
could withstand; sometimes he was mounted on a
fiery steed which few mortals could have bestrode,
and with lance in hand he was taught to tilt against
phantom knights, which, in the most desperate
encounters, he invariably overthrew. Thus, by the
time he had attained to man's estate, no knight in
Europe was so accomplished, while none surpassed
him in virtue or valour.

Meantime the Lord High Steward bitterly

mourned the loss of his promising son. In vain he sent messengers throughout the world to find him, and at last, remembering the ancient proverb, " Who wants goes, who does not want sends," he resolved to go in search of the boy himself. Storing himself with gold and precious jewels, he set off, attended only by his faithful De Fistycuff. From place to place he wandered, year after year, till his locks were turned to silvery grey, and his beard became like the down of a thistle. One evening his heart fainting, and his once firm knees trembling, he reached the gate of a monastery in Bohemia. Then he sunk down before even his Squire could ring the bell to summon the monks to his assistance. When the porter opened the door, the Lord High Steward of England had breathed his last, and poor De Fistycuff was bewailing his loved master's death, and his own hard fate, in being thus left alone in a foreign land. The monks buried Sir Albert hard by, and raised a monument, covered with some of his own jewels, over his grave, reserving the remainder to pay the expenses of his funeral. The worthy De Fistycuff they recommended to return to his native land, unless he wished to become a monk ; an honour he declined, having his faithful Grumculda waiting for him at home. So, paying a farewell visit to his master's tomb, the jewels on which he found had by enchantment been changed to glass, he set off on his journey. Happily he had, however, some of the presents intended for the wicked Kalyb in his pockets ; so, like an honest Briton, he was able to pay his way, and be no discredit to his country. Leaving him to pursue his toilsome peregrination, we return once more to the cavern of Kalyb.

CHAPTER II

EVEN the Enchantress wondered at the progress in the arts and sciences her captive was making ; but, as she knew that he was destined to become a great man, she was aware that she could not hope to stop his progress. All she could do was to keep him shut up till fate set him free. One day the friendly fairy addressed the Prince:—" Know," she said, " the Enchantress sleeps once, and once only, for one week every hundred years. Her magic art depends on her silver wand, which on that occasion she hides away so carefully that it is scarcely possible to discover it. Still, we will search. For that opportunity I have long been waiting. If we can possess ourselves of it, she will be completely in our power, and we can work our will within the magic cavern. Know also that I am an English fairy, Sabrina by name. I love you because you are kind to me, and because you come of an honest English stock. If we can overcome the Enchantress, I will enable you to commence that career of glory for which I know that your heart is even now thirsting." The young Prince's heart beat high with joy and hope on hearing these words. Anxiously they watched the Enchantress, to try and discover where she would place her silver wand. Day after day they followed her through all the vast interminable recesses of her magic cavern. Every day she grew more drowsy and less inclined to speak ; which is not surprising, considering how long she had been awake, and how sleepy she must have become.

In spite of all this vigilance, however, at last she appeared without her silver wand; and soon after they saw her sink down on a couch of rose-leaves she had prepared for herself in a sumptuous apartment, where, had it not been for her hideous countenance, where all the malignant passions were portrayed, she would have looked like a sovereign resting on her bed of state. The Prince was eager instantly to set off to look for the silver wand.

" Stay," whispered the Fairy Sabrina, " she yet sleeps with one eye open, like a weasel ; wait till she closes both, and snores." Accordingly they waited till both Kalyb's eyes were closed, and loud snores echoed along the vaulted roof. Then off they set.

" Nothing worth having can be gained without toil and trouble," observed the Dwarf, as he parted from the Prince. All the other attendants of the Enchantress had taken the opportunity to go to sleep likewise; so silence profound reigned throughout the cavern, broken only by her snores. The Prince searched and searched in every direction, under heaps of costly jewels and glittering robes, piles of gold and silver, and rich armour ; but they had now no charms for him : the silver wand which was to set him free to commence his noble career was all he sought for—that wand, the type of knowledge, which can only be obtained by study and perseverance. Day after day he sought for it; but at the end of each day all he could say was that he believed he could tell where it was not. The Dwarf came back equally unsuccessful ; but still numberless heaps had been turned over, intricate passages explored, profound depths dived into, and unthought of recesses in the cavern discovered.

Five days had thus passed away; the Prince
knew more about the cavern than he had ever
known before; the sixth day came, and that, too,
ended. He had added to his knowledge, but the
silver wand had not been found. He became
anxious, as well he might. On the seventh the
Enchantress would awake and resume her power.
More diligently than ever he searched about; the
Dwarf seconded his efforts. Before him appeared,
as he wandered on, a golden door. After many a
hearty shove he forced it open. A steep flight of
rugged stone steps led winding upwards he knew
not where. Boldly he entered, and climbed on, on,
on. Though rough and steep were the steps he
did not weary or hesitate. Sometimes the stair was
spiral, and he went round and round, and sometimes
it led him directly upwards. Scarcely a glimmer of
light enabled him to find his way; but the Dwarf
was at his heels, encouraging him, and he recollected
the silver wand of which he was in search, and
persevered. Strong and healthy as he was he
began to draw his breath quickly, when the full
light of the glorious sun burst on him, and he found
himself in a magnificent temple of alabaster, on the
summit of a lofty mountain.

From the windows of the temple he could behold
the whole surrounding country to a vast distance,
far, far beyond the forest which grew round the
base of the mountain. There were cities and
palaces, and silvery streams, and rich fields, and
glowing orchards, and meadows full of cattle, and
grassy downs covered with sheep—such a scene
as he had not beheld since his boyhood, when
Kalyb first got possession of him. He stood

contemplating it with delight. How long he might have stood it is impossible to say, when the sound of a distant church-bell was wafted up to his ears. It reminded him that the hour was approaching when the dreadful Kalyb would awake. He thought to make his escape out of the temple, but that he found was impossible ; the walls of the tower in which he stood were a hundred feet high, with pointed iron spikes below, to catch any who might fall on them. Again must he sink into the power of the cruel Kalyb? His brave heart rebelled at the thought ; he would dare and do anything to avoid it.

He spoke aloud. "You are right," said the Dwarf; "but look ! what is that?" He turned his head, and beheld before him, on a velvet cushion, which covered a marble table, the silver wand of which he had been so long in search. He grasped it eagerly.

"Follow me," said the Dwarf, hastening onward, "no time is to be lost." Down the steps they sped. "No time is to be lost," cried the Dwarf again. Faster, faster went the Prince's feet. On he rattled—on—on—often several steps at a time. Nothing stopped him. The bottom was reached ; the massive door was closed; in vain he pushed against it. He touched it with his silver wand ; open it flew. Along the vaulted passages of the cavern he sped. Many a hideous monster started up, but a wave of the silver wand put them to flight.

The Prince and his attendant reached the chamber of the Enchantress. Her snoring had ceased. She had begun to rub her eyes and move uneasily, with many a grunt and snort. She was about to awake. Who could have told what mischief one glance of her evil eye would have effected. "Strike! strike!" said the Fairy. The Prince struck the bed. Instantly loud shrieks and groans, and cries most terrific, were heard filling the air, and shouts most horrible of mocking laughter, and bellowings, and roarings, and hissings, and the walls of the chamber began to rock, and the bed began to sink, and flames burst forth, and stenches most overwhelming arose. The horrible noises increased till dense lurid vapours concealed the spot where the Enchantress's chamber had been, though her helpless cries were heard far, far down in the depths of the earth; and the Prince found himself standing in the wild cavern, but, in the place of the Dwarf, there stood a beautiful Fairy by his side. "I prepared you for a change," said the Fairy, with a smile; "but come, we are not the only ones to be set free. Let us not forget our companions in misfortune any more than those in our prosperity."

The Prince made the politest of bows, and said he was completely under the Lady Sabrina's directions. "Then come with me," she said, and led the way till they reached a vast castle of brass, with battlements and towers glittering in the sun. "Within this castle lie imprisoned six valiant knights, worthy champions of Christendom, bemoaning their hard fate, and longing to be free. Had the vile Kalyb retained her power, you would have been shut up there likewise. But know, brave Prince, as by your perseverance, valour, and judgment you have overcome her and her enchantments, it is destined that you shall become the

seventh and most renowned of all, and so I hail you
as 'St. George of merrie England.' Thus you
shall be called for ages yet to come, wherever
England's might and England's deeds throughout
the world are known." The roseate hue of
modesty suffused the cheek of the young knight
as he heard these words, and he vowed that he
would ever strive to prove worthy of the honourable
title he had received.

Then thrice he struck the gates of the brazen
castle. The portals flew open, and he and the
Fairy entering, found the six knights sitting lonely
and sad in separate chambers, not knowing what
had happened. They started as they heard the
voice of Sabrina mentioning their names.

"The first is St. Denis of France," said she.
With many a bow he rapidly sprang forward and
saluted St. George. The second, St. James of
Spain, slowly stalked on, and lifting his casque
bowed haughtily. The third, St. Anthony of
Italy, advanced more rapidly, and, with a flourish of
his helmet, gave him an embrace. St. Andrew of
Scotland, the fourth, rising from his couch, inquired
whence he had come, and whither he was going,
and thanked him for the valour he had displayed;
while St. Patrick, the fifth, almost wrung off his
hand, as he expressed his delight in meeting so
gallant a knight; and the sixth, St. David of
Wales, vowed that no pleasure could surpass what
he felt at being thus set free by a knight second
only to himself in all knightly accomplishments.
Besides the knights, six faithful squires, who had
followed their fortunes for many years, lay imprisoned in a separate dungeon. These also St.

George had the great satisfaction of setting free; when once more they rejoined their beloved masters, and assisted, as was their wont, in preparing them for their journey.

Then St. George and all the knights, following Sabrina, led the way to the stables of the castle, where stood, ready caparisoned, seven of the most superb steeds mortal eye ever beheld. " Six of them are for those brave knights," she said ; " the seventh, Bayard by name, is reserved for you ; while six other most excellent horses are for their six faithful squires."

The knights, eager to be gone, mounted their steeds, as did their squires theirs, while Sabrina conducted St. George back to the castle, where, in a chamber, hung numberless suits of the most magnificent armour. Choosing out the strongest corselet, Sabrina buckled it on his breast ; she laced on his helmet, and completely clothed him in glittering steel. Then bringing forth a mighty falchion, she placed it in his hand, and said :—" No monarch was ever clothed in richer armour. Of such strength and invincible power is your steed, that while you are on his back no knight shall be able to conquer you. Your armour is of steel so pure that no battle-axe can bruise, no weapon pierce it. Your sword, which is called Ascalon, was made by the Cyclops. It will hew asunder the hardest flint, or cut the strongest steel, and in its pummel such magic virtue lies, that neither treason nor witchcraft can prevail against you, or any violence be offered as long as you wear it."

The good fairy thus having spoken, St. George, fully caparisoned, went forth from the castle, and

mounting Bayard, prepared with the other champions to leave the Black Forest—Sabrina, in her
own chariot, drawn by ten peacocks, leading the
way. Just then a stranger appeared in sight, sad
and sorrowful, travelling on.

" De Fistycuff ! " exclaimed St. George, in a
cheerful voice, " my honest parent's faithful squire."
De Fistycuff started, as well he might, and rushed
forward. He knew the voice, but whence it had come
he could not tell. St. George tore off his corselet,
and exposed to view the green dragon on his bosom.
Thus De Fistycuff knew who it was, and, embracing
him, burst into tears. Having recovered himself,
and once more buckled on his young master's armour,
De Fistycuff mounted his steed.

Then the whole party set forward, and travelled
on till they reached the coast. Then they took
shipping, and, at St. George's particular request,
proceeded to his paternal castle, near the beautiful
city of Coventry. There having dwelt for the
space of nine months, and erected a sumptuous
monument over the grave of the hapless princess,
St. George's mother, they expressed their desire to
set forth once more in search of those noble adventures to which they had devoted their lives. St.
George, nothing loath, promised to accompany
them, and the faithful De Fistycuff entreated that
he might not be left behind ; so, all accoutred, and
lavishly supplied with everything they required, they
set forth with their faithful squires, and travelled on
till the time arrived for their separating in different
directions. What then befell them, and what
wondrous deeds they performed, shall in course
of time be told.

CHAPTER III

THE Seven Champions having crossed the British Channel to France, and traversed that lovely country, where they banqueted, to their heart's content, on fricassees and ragouts, washed down by huge draughts of Burgundy and claret, reached at length a broad plain where stood a brazen pillar. Here seven ways met, and here the noble knights, with many a flourish of their spears and not a few in their speeches, though history does not record them, parted with expressions of mutual esteem, to follow out with their faithful squires their separate adventures.

St. George, accompanied only by the faithful De Fistycuff, at once passed over to the coast of Africa, knowing full well that in that unknown land of wonders he was more likely to meet with adventures worthy of his prowess than in any other part of the world. He journeyed on for many a mile over burning sands, his polished steel armour glittering in the sun, striking terror into all beholders, and almost blinding his poor squire, who, hot and panting, followed him wearily.

Far across the plains of Africa he travelled till he reached the very ancient, though little known kingdom of Timbuctoo. King Bobadildo, the sable monarch of that empire, so wonderfully renowned in its own annals, if not in those of other countries, received him with all the courtesy due to his rank as a British knight, and the renown which the faithful De Fistycuff, who never lost an opportunity of putting in a good word for his master, stated that he intended to acquire.

The Knight was feasted sumptuously, and magnificent shows were got up for his entertainment, while the King, who had taken a great fancy to him, from believing that he would be of great use in leading his warriors to the fight against the enemies of his realm, pressed him to remain, hoping that by his falling in love with his lovely daughter he might be induced to become his son-in-law. The colour of the young princess's complexion, which was of the most sable hue, shining lustrously with palm oil, although much admired in her native country, was to the British knight an insuperable objection to a closer alliance than that of the friendship he enjoyed, though he did not say so; but stated that he was anxious to go where glory awaited him, and that all matrimonial arrangements he must defer till he had won that fame for which his heart panted.

Accordingly, the next morning, followed by De Fistycuff, who had some difficulty in buckling his belt after the good fare he had enjoyed, he set forth from the southern gate of the capital towards the unknown regions which lay beyond. The sweet Princess looked out of a turret window, and waved her coal-black hand, while tears coursed each other down her sable cheeks as she saw the Knight going away and leaving her all forlorn; for in her bright eyes not one of the neighbouring princes, nor any of her father's courtiers, could in any way be compared to the gallant St. George. Many other sweet princesses, at the various courts he visited in his travels, held the same opinion—a circumstance which caused a considerable amount of perplexity to the gentle-hearted and gallant Knight. As she gazed

she sighed, and then she sang words to the following
effect :—

"Go away, go away, oh, hard-hearted knight,
Go away to glory and fame ;
If you ever come back
You'll not find me slack
To change my state and name ! "

Much relieved by the impromptu expressions of her
feelings, she turned from the window, St. George
having disappeared among the distant sand-heaps,
and went to attend her honoured sire at his matutinal
meal.

St. George and his Squire travelled on day after
day, mounting higher and higher till they reached a
region where the heat was no longer so oppressive
as in the plains, and where scenes new and beautiful
opened on their enravished sight.

There were beautiful lakes of the clearest water,
full of fish of strange shapes and gorgeous hues,
which swam up to the surface, and gazed with
curious eyes at the strangers.   The trees and shrubs
were of the most gigantic proportions, the former
towering high into the sky, and a single leaf afford-
ing ample shade to the Knight and Squire and their
horses. So luscious and luxuriant, too, was the grass
that a few tufts were sufficient for a meal for the noble
steeds, and put such strength and spirit into them,
that, in spite of the fatigues they underwent, they
were ever ready for any task they might be called
on to perform.   Even the shrubs were so high that
they could ride beneath some of them.   Others
were covered with leaves of such thickness that a
spear could scarcely pierce them, while they were
armed with spikes of length so formidable that it

was dangerous to approach the branches, and impossible to force a passage through them. Strange, too, were the plants. Some were like a mass of twisting serpents which wriggled about and hissed as the travellers passed, and though St. George cut off their heads with his sword, they so quickly again grew up that he perceived that the attempt to destroy them was labour lost.

"So is it," he moralized, "with vicious propensities; the nature of the plant must be changed, or the branches will spring forth, and evil fruit will continually be produced." Other plants of the most fantastic shapes and most lovely hues seemed endued with life. One covering a wide circle of ground, and tinted with every colour of the rainbow, they stopped to admire. Suddenly it darted forth feelers of great length high into the air, and drew back hundreds of gay-coloured butterflies, and moths, and beetles, which were flying near.

Numerous birds also of the most gorgeous plumage, which darted down, attracted by the flies, were seized hold of and dragged within the capacious mouth of the plant.

"On, on," cried St. George, pricking forward his steed. "If we stop to admire all these separate wonders we shall never attain the great objects of our expedition." The Squire if he heard did not heed his master, for he kept gazing at the proceedings of the strange plant, and trying to count the number of insects it gobbled up in a minute. Thoughtlessly he drew closer and closer, till suddenly the monster plant darted forth all its feelers and grasped him round the body. He felt himself dragged helplessly towards the capacious

maw where he had already seen so many creatures
conveyed. "Oh, master, master! help, help!"
he shouted at the top of his voice, though a feeler
getting round his neck almost stopped his breath.

St. George, seeing what had occurred, spurred
back in hot haste, and, slashing away with his
trusty falchion, severed the feelers after vast
exertions and rescued his frightened squire.

"If you had done as I told you this would not
have happened," he observed, as he freed him from
the thick masses of sinew which surrounded his
body. "Oh, De Fistycuff, remember to do right
and what you are bid by those who know best what
is for your good, and then don't fear the consequences; but never stand gazing at what is bad or
dangerous, and fancy that you run no risk of being
drawn into the snare laid for you!"

The Squire listened respectfully to his master's
lecture, and then followed him at a humble distance,
resolving to profit by his advice.

Night with her sable wings was about to over-
spread the earth, and the tall woods resounded with
strangest cries, and shrieks, and hisses of the
wonderful wild animals which roamed through
them, when the Knight thought it high time to look
about for some place of shelter, where, free from
their attacks, he and his squire might repose till the
return of the rosy dawn would enable them to
discern their foes, and face them bravely.

A large rock appeared before them. Within it
was a cave with a rude porch in front. In this
rough habitation dwelt a hermit, whose voice they
heard bewailing the sad fate to which his country was
doomed. The Knight entered; a lamp stood on a

table in the centre of the cave. The hermit rose from his couch and welcomed St. George and De Fistycuff. He was a venerable man, with a long beard of silvery whiteness; and as he tottered forward he seemed bowed almost to the ground with the weight of years.

" Gladly will I afford you shelter and such food as my cell can furnish, most gallant Knight," he said; and, suiting the action to the word, he placed a variety of provisions on the table. " I need not inquire to what country you belong, for I see by the arms of England engraven on your burgonet whence you come. I know the knights of that land are brave and gallant, and ready to do battle in aid of the distressed. Here, then, you will find an opportunity for distinguishing yourself by a deed which will make your name renowned throughout the world."

St. George pricked up his ears at this, and eagerly inquired what it was. " This, you must understand, most noble Knight, is the renowned territory of Bagabornabou, second to none in the world in importance in the opinion of its inhabitants. None was so prosperous, none so flourishing, when a most horrible misfortune befell the land, in the appearance of a terrific green dragon, of huge proportions, who ranges up and down the country, creating devastation and dismay in every direction. No corner of the land is safe from his ravages; no one can hope to escape the consequences of his appearance. Every day his insatiable maw must be fed with the body of a young maiden, while so pestiferous is the breath which exhales from his throat that it causes a plague of a character so violent that whole districts have been depopulated by it. He commences his career of destruction at dawn every morning, and till his victim is ready he continues to ravage the land. When he has swallowed his lamentable repast he remains asleep till next morning, and then he proceeds as before.

" Many attempts have been made to capture him during the night, but they have proved as fruitless as trying to catch a weasel (if you happen to have heard of such an animal, St. George, in your travels) asleep. Fruitless I will not say to him, for he has invariably destroyed the brave men who have gone out to attack him, and has swallowed them for his supper. For no less than twenty-four long years has this dreadful infliction been suffered by our beloved country, till scarcely a maiden remains alive, nor does a brave man continue in it. The most lovely and perfect of her sex, the King's only daughter, the charming Sabra, is to be made an offering to the fell dragon to-morrow, unless a knight can be found gallant and brave enough to risk his life in mortal combat with the monster, and with skill and strength sufficient to destroy him.

" The King has promised, in his royal word, that, should such a knight appear and come off victorious, he will give him his daughter in marriage and the crown of Bagabornabou at his decease."

" Ah ! " exclaimed the English Knight, his whole countenance beaming with satisfaction, " here is a deed to be done truly worthy of my prowess ! What think you of that, reverend hermit ? " And he bared his breast, exhibiting the portrait of the green dragon which had been marked there at his birth

"A circumstance ominous of deep import," observed the Hermit, nodding his head; "either the green dragon will kill you, or you will kill the green dragon."

"Now, by my halidom, but I fully purpose to kill the dragon and rescue the Princess," cried the Knight, in a cheerful voice. "Won't we, my brave De Fistycuff?"

"What men dare they can do," answered the Squire, nodding his head, for he was very sleepy.

Accordingly, the hermit having prepared couches of leaves, the Knight and his attendant rested till the cheerful cock, true messenger of day, gave notice that the sun was about to uprise from his sandy bed. Then, springing to his feet after a hurried meal, aided by his squire and the trembling fingers of the hermit, he carefully buckled on his armour, and mounting his richly caparisoned steed, he declared himself ready for the combat. Followed by De Fistycuff, and preceded by the hermit on a mule, who went to show the way, he proceeded to the valley where the dragon was asleep, and where the King's daughter was to be offered up as a sacrifice.

As he came in sight of it his eyes rested on one of the sweetest and most lovely maidens he had ever beheld, arrayed in pure white Arabian silk, and led to the place of death by a numerous band of sage and modest matrons, who mourned with bitter tears her hard fate.

This melancholy spectacle still further stimulated the overflowing courage of the English Knight, so spurring on towards the mourning group, he assured the lovely maiden that he was prepared to battle bravely in her cause, and entreated her to return to her father's court till the result of the coming contest became known.

"He'll do it if it is to be done," observed De Fistycuff, wishing to add his mite of consolation to the ladies' hearts, and pointing to his master, who had ridden slowly on; and having thus delivered himself he spurred after him.

The daring Knight and his faithful squire now entered the valley where the terrific green dragon had his abode. No sooner did the fiery eyes of the hideous monster fall on the steel-clad warrior, instead of the fair maiden he expected to see, than from his leathern throat he sent forth a cry of rage louder and more tremendous than thunder, and arousing himself he prepared for the contest about to occur. As he reared up on his hind legs, with his wings outspread, and his long scaly tail, with a huge red fork, extending far away behind him, his sharp claws wide open, each of the size of a large ship's anchor, his gaping mouth armed with double rows of huge teeth, between which appeared a fiery red tongue, and vast eyes blazing like burning coals, while his nostrils spouted forth fire, and the upper part of his body was covered with glittering green scales brighter than polished silver, and harder than brass, the under part being of a deep golden hue, his appearance might well have made even one of the bravest of men unwilling to attack him.

St. George trembled not, but thought of the lovely Sabra, and nerved himself for the encounter. De Fistycuff did not like his looks, and had he been alone would have been tempted to beat a retreat, but his love for his master kept him by his side.

"See," said the Hermit, who had come thus far, "there is the dragon! He is a monster huge and horrible; but I believe that, like other monsters, by bravery and skill he can be overcome. See, the valley is full of fruit-trees! Should he wound you, and should you faint, you will find one bearing oranges of qualities so beneficial, that, should you be able to procure one plucked fresh from the tree, it will instantly revive you. Now, farewell! See, the brute is approaching!"

"Remember," cried St. George, turning to De Fistycuff, "this fight is to be all my own. You stand by and see fair play. Only, if I am down, and the brute dares to hit me, then rush in to my rescue." The faithful squire nodded his assent.

On came the monster dragon, flapping his wings, spouting fire from his nostrils, and roaring loudly with his mouth. St. George couched his sharp spear, and spurring his steed, dashed onward to the combat. So terrific was the shock that the Knight was almost hurled from his saddle, while his horse, driven back on his haunches, lay, almost crushed, beneath the monster's superincumbent weight; but both man and steed extricating themselves with marvellous agility, St. George made another thrust of his spear, with all his might, against the scaly breast of the dragon. He might as well have struck against a gate of brass.

In a moment the stout spear was shivered into a thousand fragments, and the dragon uttered a loud roar of derision. At the same time, to show what he could do, he whisked round his venomous pointed tail with so rapid a movement that he brought both man and horse sorely bruised to the ground.

There they lay, almost senseless from the blow, while the dragon retreated backward some hundred paces or more, with the intention of coming back with greater force than before, and completing the victory he had almost won. Happily De Fistycuff divined the monster's purpose, and seeing one of the orange-trees of which the hermit had spoken, he picked an orange and hurried with it to his master.

Scarcely had the Knight tasted it than he felt his strength revive, and leaping to his feet, he gave the remainder of it to his trusty steed, on whose back instantly mounting, he stood prepared, with his famous sword Ascalon in his hand, to receive the furious charge which the dragon was about to make.

Though his spear had failed him at a pinch, his trusty falchion was true as ever; and making his horse spring forward, he struck the monster such a blow on his golden-coloured breast that the point entered between the scales, inflicting a wound which made it roar with pain and rage.

Slight, however, was the advantage which the Knight thereby gained, for there issued forth from the wound so copious a stream of black gore, with an odour so terrible, that it drove him back, almost drowning him and his brave steed, while the noxious fumes, entering their nostrils, brought them both fainting and helpless to the ground.

De Fistycuff, mindful of his master's commands, narrowly eyed the dragon, to see what he was about to do. Staunching his wound with a touch of his fiery tail, he flapped his green wings, roaring hoarsely, and shook his vast body, preparatory to another attack on the Knight.

" Is that it ? " cried the Squire ; and running to the orange-tree, whence he plucked a couple of the golden fruit, he poured the juice of one down the throat of his master, and of the other down that of Bayard. Both revived in an instant, and St. George, springing on Bayard's back, felt as fresh and ready for the fight as ever. Both had learned the importance of avoiding the dragon's tail, and when he whisked it on one side Bayard sprang to the other, and so on backwards and forwards, nimbly avoiding the blows aimed by the venomous instrument at him or his rider.

Again and again the dragon reared itself up, attempting to drop down and crush his gallant assailant ; but Bayard, with wonderful sagacity comprehending exactly what was to be done, sprung backwards or aside each time the monster descended, and thus avoided the threatened catastrophe. Still the dragon appeared as able as ever to endure the combat. St. George saw that a strenuous effort must be made, and taking a fresh grasp of Ascalon, he spurred onward to meet the monster, who once more advanced, with outstretched wings, with the full purpose of destroying him. This time St. George kept his spurs in the horse's flanks. " Death or victory must be the result of this charge," he shouted to De Fistycuff.

With Ascalon's bright point kept well before him, he drove directly at the breast of the monster. The sword struck him under the wing ; through the thick flesh it went, and nothing stopped it till it pierced the monster's heart. Uttering a loud groan, which resounded through the neighbouring woods and mountains, and made even the wild beasts tremble with consternation, the furious green dragon fell over on its side, when St. George, drawing his falchion from the wound, dashed on over the prostrate form of the monster, and, ere it could rise to revenge itself on its destroyer, with many a blow he severed the head from the body. So vast was the stream which flowed forth from the wound that the whole valley speedily became a lake of blood, and the river which ran down from it first gave notice, by its sanguineous hue, to the inhabitants of the neighbouring districts that the noble Champion of England had slain their long tormenting enemy.

The victorious Knight now refreshed himself and his steed with a couple of the oranges which De Fistycuff brought him, and which completely restored them to the vigour with which they began the combat. He then stuck the huge head of the once terrific dragon on a truncheon, which was formed by his faithful Squire out of the handle of the spear, the head of which had been shivered against the scaly sides of the monster at the commencement of the combat.

Having delivered the trophy of his prowess to De Fistycuff, to be borne before him, he rode on towards the capital of the kingdom, where he expected to be welcomed by the lovely Sabra, to be received by the sovereign and his people as a conqueror, to have heard all the bells in the empire ringing, and to have seen every house illuminated, and bonfires blazing in every street. He had to learn the bitter lesson that success frequently only creates enemies and detractors.

Now, there was residing at the court of King Battabolo, the sovereign of Bagabornabou, Almidor,

the black King of Morocco, who had long in vain
sought the hand of the Princess Sabra. For many
reasons she could not abide him; and now, when he
heard of the successful combat of St. George with
the dragon, he knew that he should have less chance
than ever of winning her love. With baseness
unparalleled he resolved to make one desperate
effort to gain her. Accordingly, he, by the most
extensive promises, engaged the services of twelve
warriors of renown to waylay the British Champion,
in order to deprive him of his trophy and of his life,
intending to present himself before the fair Sabra, and
to boast that he had himself destroyed the dragon.

Passing through a narrow defile, St. George
beheld the twelve African knights flourishing their
swords, and prepared to intercept his progress.

"Take charge of Bayard," quoth he to De
Fistycuff; "I'll meet these recreants sword in
hand on foot." Thus speaking, he drew Ascalon
from the scabbard, and advanced towards his foes.
From the narrowness of the defile only three could
engage in the fight at once. Sharply clashed the
steel. Loud rang their swords upon his polished
armour; but Ascalon soon found an entrance
through their coats of mail, and one after the other
fell breathless to the ground. Three more then
came on; but standing on the bodies of the
prostrate steeds, he with one stroke of his falchion
severed their heads from their bodies, which rolled
over in the ensanguined dust. With three equal
downward strokes he cut in two, from the crown to
the saddle, the next three which advanced, while
the remainder turning to fly, he pierced them with
Ascalon ignominiously through the back.

Almidor had all the time stood on the summit of a mountain hard by to witness the defeat of the British Champion; but when he saw that instead he remained victor of the field, he hastened back to the city to announce the death of the dragon by the sword of the strange Knight. Pen might fail to do justice to the magnificent preparations made to do honour to the brave Champion who had conquered the Green Dragon. As he approached the city he was met by a sumptuous chariot of massive gold, drawn by fifty milk-white steeds ; the wheels were of the purest ebony, and the covering was of silk embossed with gold. On either side rode a hundred of the noblest peers of Bagabornabou, attired in crimson velvet, and mounted on chargers of the same pure colour as those which drew the chariot. Stepping into the chariot, while De Fistycuff led Bayard with one hand, and carried aloft the dragon's head with the other, he entered the city amid strains of delicious and martial music, and beneath banners and embroidered tapestry and rich arras waving from every window, from which looked down thousands of bright eyes to admire him. But none were so bright as those of the beauteous Sabra, who welcomed him in a rich pavilion prepared for his reception, where he laid at her feet the trophies of his prowess ; and as she gazed at the dragon's monstrous jaws she shuddered to think that she might have had to go down them, and felt her gratitude and eke a warmer feeling increase for the gallant stranger who had preserved her from a fate so terrible.

Here all the first physicians in the land stood around with precious salves to dress his wounds,

and administer specifics against the effects of the
dragon's poisonous breath and venom. The
Knight, having requested that they might all be
left by his bed-side, and that he might be left alone,
aided by De Fistycuff, emptied them all out of the
window, and having declared himself next morning
infinitely better, thereby gained immense popularity
among the disciples of Æsculapius, who each rested
under the pleasing belief that his own nostrum had
worked the cure.

CHAPTER IV

No sooner had the blushing morn displayed her
beauties in the east, and gilded with her radiant
beams the mountain tops, than Sabra repaired to
the Champion's pavilion, and presented him with a
diamond ring of inestimable value, which she prayed
him to wear on his finger, not only as an ornament,
but because it was endued with many excellent and
occult virtues.

That day the British Champion was entertained
with one of the most magnificent banquets that had
ever taken place in Africa. Ample justice was
done to it by all present, especially by De Fistycuff,
who eat away most heartily, and quaffed down huge
beakers of rosy wine—all, as he declared, for the
honour of Old England. Ere the feast was ended,
Almidor, the black King of Morocco, under pre-
tence of doing honour to the Christian Knight, rose
from his seat, and presented him with a bowl of
Samian wine. The noble Champion took it,
thoughtless of treachery; but as he lifted it to his

lips the magic ring touched the rim, when, to the astonishment of all present, it shivered into a thousand fragments. The Princess Sabra shrieked out that some vile treachery was intended; but so firm was the confidence of the King, her father, in the honour of Almidor, that he refused to credit the accusation.

Thus a second time was St. George saved from the machinations of his enemy. Like a lynx, however, Almidor watched for another opportunity of gratifying his hatred.

In tournaments, dances, and other heroic exercises, the Champion passed his time, until the faithful De Fistycuff reminded him that he was sadly wasting it, if he wished to gain a name to be handed down to posterity. "You are right, my faithful monitor," he answered, " I'll bid farewell to the Princess, and be gone."

The Knight found out Sabra seated in a bower of jessamine. He told her his errand. " Refuse not," she replied, " my dear, loved lord of England, her who, for thy sake, would leave parents, country, and the inheritance of the crown of Bagabornabou, and would follow thee as a pilgrim through the wide world. The sun shall sooner lose his splendour, the pale moon drop from her orb, the sea forget to ebb and flow, and all things change their course, than Sabra prove inconstant to St. George of England. Let, then, the priest of Hymen knit that gordian knot, the knot of wedlock, which death alone has power to untie."

The Champion, suddenly recollecting that it was leap year, and delighted with the maiden who had so ably put in a word in her own favour, allowed his heart, which had never before beat with any other passion but that of arms, to yield to the tender one of love. Yet, willing to try her longer, he replied—" Sweet Princess, not content that I have risked my life to preserve yours, would you have me sacrifice my honour, give over the chase of dazzling glory, lay all my warlike trophies in a woman's lap, and change my truncheon for a distaff? No, Sabra, George of England was born in a country where true chivalry is nourished, and hath sworn to see the world, as far as the lamp of heaven can lend him light, before he is fettered in the golden chains of wedlock. Why decline the suit of King Almidor, fit consort for one of your high rank?"

" Because," she replied, with a curl of her lip, " the fell King of Morocco is more bloody-minded than a crocodile, but thou gentle as a lamb; his tongue more ominous of ill than that of a screeching night owl, but thine sweeter than the morning lark; his touch more odious than that of a venomous serpent, but thine more pleasant than that of the curling vine."

" But stay, Princess," put in St. George; " I am a Christian—you a Pagan."

" I've thought of that," she replied. " I will forsake my country's gods, and, like you, become a Christian." Saying this she broke a golden ring, giving, as a pledge of her love, one-half to the Knight, and keeping the other herself.

Thereon St. George, resisting no longer, owned his love, and promised, on his knightly word, to come back when he had achieved a few more heroic deeds and wed her.

The treacherous Almidor, hiding behind the

jessamine bower, had overheard all the uncomplimen-
tary references to himself, and, burning with a desire
of vengeance, hastened to the King, and told him
that his daughter intended quitting the faith of her
ancestors and flying with the Christian Knight.
This so enraged the King that, yielding to the
suggestions of the wicked Almidor, he agreed to
send him, with treacherous intent, to the court
of Egypt, as bearer of a sealed letter, in which
document he entreated King Ptolemy to take an
early opportunity of destroying one who was a
despiser and uprooter of their ancient belief.   Summoning St. George, with expressions of great
esteem, while Almidor stood at his right hand,
glancing unutterable hatred from his large eyes, the
King informed him that to do him honour he would
send him as an ambassador to the court of the
magnificent Sovereign of Egypt, a country in which
he was sure to meet with adventures worthy of his
arms.

The true-hearted Knight fell into the trap, and,
dazzled with the thought of fresh adventures, agreed
to set forth.   Summoning De Fistycuff, he buckled
on his armour, and set out towards the rising of the
sun.   Many adventures he met with ; many monsters
he slew.   On approaching the famed river Nile,
De Fistycuff, weary with the heat, sat himself down
on what he took to be the trunk of a large tree,
fastening the bridle of his steed to, as he believed,
one of the branches, while his master was scouring
over the plain after a troop of tawny lions, which
had been committing great depredations in the
neighbouring lands.   Sleep overtook the Squire.
He slept he knew not how long, when he was

awoke by the loud snorts and cries of his steed, and by finding himself borne along in a most uneasy manner. What was his horror, on opening his eyes, to discover a huge head, with terrific jaws, projecting from the seeming log before him, snapping at everything as it moved swiftly towards the broad stream of the Nile, while his horse, frantic with terror, was tugging at the bridle behind, in vain attempting to get loose, or stop the progress of the monster, which was one of the largest of the crocodiles of that famed stream, and held in especial reverence by the heathen priests of that district! The Squire dared not jump off, for fear of being trampled on by the hind feet of the brute, nor could he, for reasons into which most stout squires will enter, leap on to his horse's back and cut the bridle, so he sat still, waving and shouting to St. George to come to his assistance. At last, St. George, having killed a dozen of the lions, beheld the peril of his faithful follower, and spurred onward to his aid. Charging with a new spear, which had been presented to him by the matrons of Bagabornabou, as a mark of their admiration of his prowess in having slain the dragon, he bore down upon the crocodile. He charged directly at its mouth, and inflicted a deep wound in its throat The monster snapped its jaws, hoping to bite off the spear-head; but the Knight was too quick for him, and again had his spear ready for another thrust. Again he charged, putting out the brute's right eye; and the third time he charged the left was driven in. All the time the crocodile was wriggling his tail, greatly to the terror of the horse and the discomfort of De Fistycuff, who found himself every moment borne nearer and nearer to the Nile. "One charge more, and you shall be safe," cried the Knight; and, true to his word, his spear entered the monster's heart, and it rolled over, very nearly, however, crushing the faithful Squire by its weight. Scarcely had De Fistycuff been liberated by his kind master's aid, and set on his steed, than there sallied forth from a heathen temple hard by a procession of priests, some walking under silk or velvet canopies of crimson or yellow, or blue and gold; others swinging censers of incense; and others bearing aloft on platforms large images of white bulls and apes, and snakes and crocodiles, while gay banners floated in the air. When they beheld the huge monster just slain they all set up loud lamentations, bitterly cursing whoever had destroyed this their god.

"Now, by my halidom, this is more than I can bear!" cried St. George. "On, De Fistycuff, on! Down with the infidels!"

With this shout he and his Squire rode in among them, overthrowing their canopies and images, tearing down their banner, and putting the priests and their followers to flight.

King Ptolemy, having heard of this deed, sent forth a hundred of his best warriors, to bring before him in chains the audacious strangers; but St. George treated them much the same as he did the knights of Bagabornabou, and not one returned alive to tell of their defeat.

Then he rode on to the city of Memphis, to deliver his letter. Weary and faint from his fatigues, instead of meeting with the reception he had a right to expect, he and his Squire found themselves surrounded by the whole populace of the city, set on by the King and his ministers. The gates were shut. Brickbats and tiles came showering down on their heads. In vain they charged right and left. Aided by a thousand warriors, clad in chain armour, the infuriated populace, threatening vengeance on the despisers of their religion, hemmed them in. De Fistycuff was torn from his horse. St. George, after performing feats of unheard-of valour, was ignominiously dragged from his, and borne, faint and bleeding, into the presence of the King.

" Is this the way you treat strangers ? " exclaimed he, indignantly. " I came to your country as an ambassador. Here are my credentials ; " and, drawing the letter from the lining of his helmet, he presented it in due form.

" Ah! ah! what you are your deeds and this letter show," cried King Ptolemy, stamping with rage. " You despise our ancient religion, and would make converts of our people. Bear him and his attendant off to prison."

The King pondered all night how he should destroy the strangers, and he resolved to make them join in combat with a hundred of the fiercest lions ever collected, to make sport for his subjects. The day arrived when the dreadful combat was to take place, and thousands of people assembled in the vast amphitheatre built for the purpose, to which even the huge pyramids seemed as pismires' nests.

St. George claimed the right of having his sword and steed; and the King, little dreaming of the courage and sagacity of Bayard, and the virtues which existed in Ascalon, and believing that, although a few lions might be killed thereby, greater sport would be afforded to his people, as he had no doubt the rest would easily tear him from his horse, and crush him in his armour, granted his request.

With a flourish of trumpets the Knight and his Squire entered the arena. De Fistycuff kept carefully behind his master. With terrific roars the hundred lions rushed in at once, amidst the loud plaudits of the spectators. On they bounded towards the Knight. Ascalon was in his hand. One after the other their heads fell, severed from their tawny bodies by the trusty steel. The Squire's chief labour was to keep them off Bayard's tail, lest, when he flung his heels out behind, the Champion's aim might be less certain. The plaudits of the spectators were changed to groans of rage when they saw the carcasses of their favourite lions, who had already swallowed so many thousand slaves, strewing the wide arena. They shouted loudly to have an end put to the pleasant pastime.

"Fair play!" cried De Fistycuff, in return brandishing his sword. "In the name of my noble master, I demand fair play!"

And St. George went on riding round and round, and slashing away with Ascalon, till he had slain every one of the hundred lions.

The treacherous King, fearing what might occur should so brave a champion wander freely through his dominions, had, in the meantime, summoned five thousand chosen warriors, and charged them to bring the Knight, dead or alive, bound before him. Scarcely was the last lion killed than they rushed into the arena, and before he and his squire had time to offer any effectual resistance, they had borne him to the ground. Then, throwing chains of steel around him, they carried him, helpless as an infant, before the King. Thence, without form of trial, he was cast into a dungeon, so massive that no strength could break through it. There, guarded night and day by lynx-eyed warders, he languished for many long years, his only companion being the faithful De Fistycuff; their chief subject of conversation being the deeds that they had done, and the wonders they had seen, and the deeds they would do, and the wonders they hoped to see.

There we must leave them, to tell what became of the Princess Sabra. In vain she waited and pined for the return of her gallant and true knight, St. George. He came not, because, as has been seen, he could not, while the black King of Morocco, with every art he could devise, prosecuted his hateful suit. Whether or not he might have succeeded is doubtful, when one night, as the Princess slept on her couch she dreamed that St. George appeared, not, as she had seen him, in shining armour, with his burgonet of glittering steel, and crimson plume of spangled feathers, but in overworn and simple attire, with pale countenance and emaciated form; and thus he spoke:—

" Sabra, I am betray'd for love of thee,
  And lodged in cave as dark as night,
From whence in vain I seek—ah! woe is me!—
  To fly and revel in thy beauteous sight.
Remain thou true and constant for my sake,
  That of my absence none may vantage take.

" Let tyrants know, if ever I obtain
  The freedom lost by treason's wicked guile,
False Afric's scourge I ever will remain,
  And turn to streaming blood Morocco's soil;
That hateful Prince of Barbary shall rue
  The just reward which is his treason's due."

These words so encouraged the Princess that when she awoke she went to her sire, and entreated him, with scalding tears, to dismiss Almidor from his court, and to allow her to enjoy that single blessedness for which she professed to have for the present so ardent an admiration. The King at length, softened by her grief, consented to her request, and, with many courteous expressions, informed the black Monarch that his daughter had finally resolved to decline his proposals. This announcement created the greatest fury in the breast of Almidor.

Calling around him all the knights and the numerous other attendants who had followed him to the court of Bagabornabou, he told them that, as he had been insulted and deceived, he was determined to be revenged.

With loud cries and burning brands the treacherous Moors that night attacked the palace where they had been long hospitably entertained, and, amid the confusion, Almidor, seizing the Princess, bore her off on his coal-black charger. In vain her father with his warriors pursued. The fierce Almidor galloped with his captive across the burning sands, which none but Moorish steed could traverse at the speed he went. Hatred, not love, animated his bosom, and thus, instead of wedding her as he had purposed, he cast her into a dark dungeon, where, her beauteous charms concealed from the light of day, she for many a long and anxious year bewailed her pitiable and cruel fate. Happily, ere she left her father's home, a kind fairy, knowing full well what was to be her fate, had presented her with a golden chain of most rare workmanship. Seven

days had it been steeped in tiger's blood, and seven
nights in dragon's milk, by which it had attained
such excellent virtue, that, as the fairy told her, if
she wore it wrapped seven times round her alabaster
neck, it would preserve her from all violence, and
enable her to retain that enchanting beauty which
had won the noble Champion's heart, and brought
so many suitors to her feet.   Thus armed, she
feared not even the fierce Almidor's cruelty.

CHAPTER V

ON parting from his comrades, the gallant Champion
of France, the famed St. Denis, attended by his
squire, Le Crapeau, wandered away through many
lands, slaying many hideous monsters, terrible wild
beasts, and frightful giants, combating in many tournaments, and paying his devoirs to many fair princesses,
as well as other maidens of high and low degree, in
which latter employment he was closely imitated by
his admiring Squire, who jocosely spoke of his
master as "that gay young Knight who laughs and
rides away."   At length he reached a magnificent
castle in Asia, surrounded by a forest of trees of
every conceivable hue, and bearing fruits tempting
to the eye and luscious to the taste.

"If the outside is so attractive, what must the
inside be!" quoth he to Le Crapeau.   "Marbleu!
but we'll knock and see."

Thereupon the Squire blew the horn which hung
at the iron gate; but instead of its being opened by
a burly porter, or by a steel-clad warrior, a troop of
fair damsels appeared, who, with sweet smiles,

invited the Knight to enter, and told him that they would conduct him to their mistress. Joyfully he followed them, when, in a superb hall, he beheld, seated on an ivory throne, glittering with diamonds of the purest water, a lady of beauty more radiant than possessed by any of the many he counted among his acquaintance. With agile steps, and many a bow and flourish of his helmet, followed nimbly by Le Crapeau, he approached the lady, and knelt at her feet.

" Rise, rise, brave Knight! I have heard of your fame and the gallant deeds you have done, and gladly I welcome you to my humble castle," said the lady, with a smile so sweet that it went right through the tender heart of St. Denis. He bowed, as did his Squire, and assured the lady that she was in no way deceived by the reports which had reached her ears, but that what they had done was as nothing compared with what they purposed to do, and would do most assuredly.

A magnificent banquet then suddenly appeared, spread out in the hall across which they had lately passed, and strains of softest music broke forth to give notice that the feast was ready. The lady, led by the Knight, approached the table, and he took his seat by her side, while Le Crapeau stood behind his chair, as in duty bound, to serve him.

" We should have guests to meet you," said the lady, " but I live alone, and your arrival was somewhat sudden, though not unexpected. I have sent forth to summon some to appear at a ball by-and-bye, as I fancy it is an entertainment in which your countrymen delight."

" Oui, Madam," cried Le Crapeau, making a

pirouette expressive of his delight; "you will see what my master and I can do when the time comes."

Thus, with agreeable and lively conversation, ample justice was done to the feast, which was composed of the lightest and most delicate viands, such as the Knight vowed he had not tasted since he had left his native land.

While the Knight lay back in his chair, to luxuriate on the thought of the pleasure his palate had enjoyed, the banqueting-table disappeared, and when he looked up, troops of gallant knights, in silk attire, and fair dames, clad in the most dazzling garments, were entering the hall. Up sprang the Knight, and, offering his hand to the lady, he led her forth to the centre of the hall, where, to the admiration of all beholders, and very much to his own satisfaction, he performed a minuette never surpassed in all Asia. Le Crapeau, meantime, seeing another damsel of radiant beauty, inferior only to that of the lady of the castle, led her forth, and bounded away, round and round the hall, to strains of the most inspiriting and lively music. His only perplexity was discovering that his fair partner did not speak; indeed, although all the knights and ladies danced in the most lively way, closely imitating the two Frenchmen, not a sound escaped their lips. A variety of dances succeeded, in all of which the Knight and his Squire excelled all competitors; nor did the festivities cease till the rosy dawn appearing in the eastern sky, the guests disappeared as silently as they had entered from the hall, and the lady and the Knight and his Squire remained its sole occupants. Le Crapeau's partner was the last to quit it, and as he rushed after her to utter a tender adieu, instead of the lady, his nose came with such force in contact with a pillar that he was sent sprawling backwards into the hall.

" Never mind," said the lady, as he picked himself up, " you will see her to-morrow, and then remember the lesson you have just received, and don't talk nonsense to her."

A dozen very ugly little black dwarfs, bearing torches in their hands, now made their appearance, and conducted the Knight to a magnificent couch prepared for him, while another stood in an adjoining room, ready for Le Crapeau, after he had performed the duty of disrobing his master. The dwarfs meantime placed themselves at the door, and intimated that they would remain there to watch over the strangers while they slumbered.

After a matutinal meal of delicacies, of which even the Knight had never heard, the lady conducted him through the castle, and exhibited to him statues, and pictures, and gems most rare and beautiful, and then she led him through gardens full of flowers, shrubs, and trees, of forms and hues and scents most strange and lovely and sweet. Thus occupied, the banqueting time arrived, followed by a ball as on the previous evening.

Unhappily, Le Crapeau, forgetting the warning he had received, followed his partner as before, when a hand, coming suddenly out of the wall, gave him so severe a cuff upon the cheek that for many minutes he lay unable to move, when at length, much crest-fallen, he slowly crept back to his post behind his master.

Thus the days passed away. Sometimes the lady

led the Knight forth, mounted on cream-coloured steeds; at others, in a chariot drawn by twenty beautiful peacocks; at others, they glided over the surface of a lake in a barge, towed by thirty milk-white swans, and visited scenes of the most enchanting beauty.

At length, however, the Knight began to weary of the monotony of his existence, and to sigh for fresh adventures and more excitement. The Squire, too, wished for change, and was not altogether pleased with the buffet he regularly got every evening at the termination of the ball.

"A parting scene is always painful," exclaimed the Knight.

"It is," answered the Squire. "I understand your wishes. I will have the steeds ready, and at early dawn we will ride forth, and leave a sweet-scented billet to thank the lady for her courtesy, and to inform her of our departure."

Less difficulty occurred in the execution of the design than might have been expected, and, rejoicing in their liberty, the Knight and his Squire rode gaily forth towards the confines of Armenia.

"But we have got well out of that," quoth the Squire to his master. "By my faith, I like more animation, less formality, and greater variety than we enjoyed down there."

"You speak the truth, my Le Crapeau; yet she was a sweet creature, that lady of the castle."

Now, the lady of the castle was no other than a powerful fairy, very kind and very woman-like, who had conceived an affection for the French Champion, when she chanced to see him as he journeyed through her realm. Even good fairies will inflict a punishment.

By means for which they could not account, the Knight and his Squire lost their way. Round and round they wandered among hills and forests, till hunger almost drove them to despair, when they were compelled to sustain nature on the berries and wild fruits which they could pluck from the trees and shrubs, and on the roots which they dug up with the points of their swords. After living many months on this hard fare a mulberry-tree, loaded with luscious fruit, appeared before them.

"Ah!" exclaimed St. Denis, "on this at least we may banquet with some pleasure;" and filling his casque with the fruit, his example being imitated by Le Crapeau, they sat themselves down, with their head-pieces between their legs, to indulge, to their heart's content, in the unexpected treat.

The Knight, who eat more leisurely than his Squire, had scarcely finished his portion when he heard a loud bray close to him, and looking round, instead of his Squire, to his amazement he beheld a starved-looking donkey standing near him, and poking his nose into Le Crapeau's now empty casque.

While yet wondering and mechanically finishing his mulberries, he felt a very uncomfortable sensation coming over his own head and legs. He rose from the ground and shook himself, but instead of the accustomed rattle of his steel armour no sound was produced. He wished to scratch his nose, but his arms appeared kept down before him. He tried to call Le Crapeau, but instead of his manly voice, which had so often shouted loudly in the battle, a timid cry alone proceeded from his throat. He looked at the donkey, and the donkey looked at him, and shook its head with an expression truly mournful. Something strange must have occurred he feared.

Wherever he went the donkey followed. He wandered away from the mulberry-tree till he reached a lake of crystal water; he approached it, when, on its mirror-like surface, instead of a steel-clad warrior, he beheld a deer with long antlers and shaggy hide, he started back with dismay. When hunger pressed him he found himself cropping the grass or thrusting his nose into the purling brook, with his attendant donkey ever by his side. Pitiable as was St. George's condition that of St. Denis was infinitely worse.

Thus for many years he continued unable to recover his natural form. Often he returned to the mulberry-tree, the cause, as he believed, of his misfortune. It did not occur to him that the fairy, whose hospitality he had enjoyed, had anything to do with it. Once, as he came to the tree, so enraged was he that he ran his horns against it and nearly broke them. His attendant donkey did the same, and not having the same protection to his scull, he received a blow so severe that he was sent reeling backwards till he sunk exhausted on the ground. St. Denis was a second time going to butt, when he heard a hollow voice breathe forth from the trunk the following words:—

" Cease to lament, thou famous man of France,
    With gentle ears, oh, listen to my moan!
Once on a time it was my fatal chance
    To be the proudest maid that ere was known.
      By birth I am the daughter of a king,
    Though now a breathless tree and senseless thing.

" My pride was such that Heaven confounded me—
  A goddess in my own conceit I was:
  What nature lent too base I thought to be,
  But deem'd myself all others to surpass.
      And therefore nectar and ambrosia sweet,
      The food of demigods, for me I counted meet.

" My pride despised the finest bread of wheat,
  And richer food I daily sought to find ;
  Refined gold was boil'd up with my meat,
  Such self-conceit my senses all did blind.
      For which the cruel fates transformed me,
      From human substance to this senseless tree.

" Seven years in shape of stag thou must remain,
  And then a purple rose, by magic's firm decree,
  Shall bring thee to thy former shape again,
  And end at last thy woeful misery :
      When this is done, be sure you cut in twain
      This fatal tree, wherein I do remain."

The Knight almost fainted when he heard these
strange words, and understood the length of time
he was to remain in his transformed condition. His
attendant donkey had also heard the words, and
treasured them up in his memory. Every day,
while his master slept, he ranged the country round,
searching for the purple rose, but every evening
returned as wise as he set out. Thus the seven
years passed mournfully away.

One day, unmindful how the time had sped, as
he trotted on, every now and then stopping and
uttering a melancholy bray, his nostrils scented the
fragrance of some roses ; and though his first im-
pulse was to eat them, on examining them more
closely, he observed that they were of lustrous
beauty and of a purple hue. Plucking a number of
them, he trotted back to St. Denis. He would

have brayed with delight, but, had he done so, he would have dropped the roses, so he restrained himself till he had laid them before his master's nose. Instantly the Knight began to devour them, as did the faithful donkey, when, a stupor coming over them, they couched down on the green-sward.

Presently extraordinary sensations came over them both, and the horns and hoofs began to loosen, and the skin to roll up in folds, and a refreshing shower falling, both Knight and Squire, on opening their eyes, discovered, to their infinite satisfaction, that they were no longer brute beasts, but that they had recovered their former comely shapes, and that their hairy hides lay vacant on the ground. Near them were their arms, now sadly in want of polishing, while their trusty steeds, long roaming the rich pastures around, no sooner beheld than recognizing them, trotted up to bear them once more to the field of battle or of fame.

Their first care was to burnish up their armour and their weapons. For many a weary hour they rubbed.

" We might have saved ourselves all this trouble, and spent the last seven years more pleasantly and profitably, had we not idled away our time in the magnificent castle of that beautiful lady down there," observed St. Denis, as he scrubbed away.

" Certes, Master dear, it's a failing I for one have when I get into the society of the fair sex, I feel little inclination to leave them ; but we have had a pretty sharp lesson, and I hope to amend for the future."

The task was performed at last. Then the

Champion, recollecting what the mulberry-tree had said, drew his sword, and with one blow cut the stout trunk quite asunder.

Instantly there issued forth a bright flame, from the midst of which appeared a lovely damsel, clothed in a robe of yellow silk, made from the cocoons of the innumerable silk-worms, which fed on the tree.

"Oh, most sweet and singular ornament of nature!" exclaimed the Knight, bowing low before her, as did his Squire; "fairer than the feathers of the graceful swan, and far more beautiful than Aurora's morning countenance, to thee, the fairest of all fair ones, most humbly and only to thy beauty do I here submit my affections. Tell me, therefore, to whom my heart must pay its true devotions, thy birth, parentage, and name."

The maiden, to whom it was long since such words had been addressed, was highly delighted with them, and informed the Knight that her name was Eglantine, that she was the daughter of the King of the neighbouring country, Armenia, and assured him that he would be welcomed at her father's court.

It is not recounted how many ferocious giants and furious lions he and Le Crapeau slew on the road while escorting the princess, though they were very numerous. They put to flight also a whole army of Pagans, who came to carry off their precious charge. Le Crapeau himself, however, took care not to omit the details, nor did St. Denis pass them by in silence. The King of Armenia, who had long mourned his daughter as lost to him for ever, was so grateful to the French Knight that

he at once promised her to him in marriage, and
entertained him with the most sumptuous banquets
and balls, and other pleasant divertisements which
his court could produce.

CHAPTER VI

St. James, the Champion of Spain, on parting from
his comrades at the brazen pillar, took ship, and
was wrecked on the coast of Sicily.

Travelling through the island, followed by his
Squire, Pedrillo, he reached the foot of Etna, then
terrifically spouting forth vast masses of flame and
boiling metal, and ashes, and smoke. Unappalled
by the sight, he climbed the mountain's height,
where, perched on a pinnacle of rock, appeared a
mighty bird, with fiery pinions—a winged phœnix.
No sooner did the monster see him than, darting
down, it attacked him with its red-hot beak, for
having dared thus to enter its dominions.

St. James drew his trusty falchion, and, whirling
it round his head, kept the fearful beak from
approaching his helmet, for well he knew that one
thrust from its deadly point would pierce through
steel and skull as easily as a lady's bodkin through
her kerchief.

The fearful combat lasted for many hours, till the
monster, hopeless of triumph, flew back to its nest
within the crater's fiery bosom.

The following day the fight was renewed, while
the faithful Pedrillo stood at a distance, counting his
rosaries, and called loudly on all the saints to aid his
master. At length the Knight and the monster,

seeing that no profit or glory was to be acquired retired, by mutual consent, from the combat.

St. James then passed into Africa, where, passing through a region infested by monsters, he slew so many that the inhabitants wished to adopt him as their Sovereign.

Crossing the Red Sea, he was once more shipwrecked, when, had not a troop of mermaids carried him and his Squire, with their horses and furniture to the shore, they would all have been drowned.

At length he reached the beautiful city of Ispahan, the capital of Persia. As he stood gazing on her fortified walls, built of pure silver; on her towers of jasper and ebony; on her glittering spires of gold and precious stones; on her houses of marble and alabaster, the streets between which were paved with tin—he heard the cheerful echoes of a thousand brazen trumpets, and saw issuing from the brazen gates a hundred armed knights, bearing blood-red streamers in their hands, and riding on as many coal-black coursers; then came the Shah, guarded by a hundred tawny Moors, with bows, and darts feathered with ravens' wings; and after them rode Celestine, the Shah's fair daughter, mounted on an unicorn, and guarded by a hundred Amazonian dames, clad in green silk. In her hand was a javelin of silver, while her fair bosom was shielded by a breastplate of gold, artificially wrought with the scales of a crocodile. A vast concourse of gentlemen and squires followed, some on horseback and some on foot.

Thus Nebazaradan, the Shah of Persia, rode forth with his daughter to the chase.

The country had been terribly overrun with wild

beasts, and the Knight heard it proclaimed that the Shah would give a corselet of finest steel, inlaid with gold, to whomsoever killed the first wild beast that day.

" Come," cried St. James, " let us after the savage beasts, and win the corselet ! "

Away scoured the Knight and his Squire over the plain till they reached a forest, in the confines of which they beheld a monstrous wild boar, devouring the remains of some passengers he had slain. The eyes of the brute sparkled like a furnace ; his tusks were sharper than spikes of steel ; and the breath, as it issued from his nostrils, seemed like a whirlwind ; his bristles looked like so many spear-heads, and his tail was like a wreath of serpents.

St. James blew his silver horn, which hung by a green silk scarf to the pommel of his saddle. The blast aroused the boar, who made at him furiously. His spear shivered against its bristly hide into a hundred fragments, when, leaping from his steed, which he directed Pedrillo to hold, he drew his falchion of Toledo steel, and valiantly on foot assailed the monster. From side to side he sprung to avoid its fearful tusks ; but in vain did the point of his weapon seek an entrance to its case-hardened flesh. At last, unslinging his battle-axe, he clove the head of the monster down to the mouth, and with a second blow cut it completely off ; then placing it on the staff of his spear, he ordered Pedrillo to bear it behind him.

Thus, riding on, he met the Shah and his daughter. The Shah at first was highly pleased with his prowess ; but when he heard that he was a

Christian Knight, his admiration was turned to rage, and he informed him that he must either become a Pagan worshipper of the sun or quit the country.

The Knight proudly answered that no one should make him quit the country unless of his own free will.

On this the Shah's army surrounded him and Pedrillo, and, after a desperate resistance on their parts, bore them to the ground.

"Now, Sir Knight, what will you do?" sneered the Shah. "However, you have killed the greatest boar in the country, and, as your reward, you shall choose the manner in which you and your Squire will be put to death."

The Champion, who was gallant on all occasions, replied that he would be shot to death by the fair damsels he had seen going forth to the chase. But when they were informed of this, none were found willing to undertake the cruel office.

This so enraged the Shah, that he ordained that they should cast lots to decide who should perform the task. The lot fell on Celestine and one of her maidens. She was to kill the Knight, and her maiden Pedrillo. Instead, however, of death's fatal instrument, a steel-tipped arrow, she shot a sigh—true messenger of love—as did her maiden; and then she hastened to her father to entreat him, with bitter, scalding tears, to liberate the strangers. At last he yielded, on condition that they should forthwith quit the country.

Already had St. James commenced his homeward journey, when, looking back on the towers of Ispahan, so inflamed was his heart with the love of Celestine, that he resolved to return and win her.

He and Pedrillo, therefore, staining their skins with the juice of some black berries, and at the same time habiting themselves in the costume of Moors, pretending to be dumb, returned to the city.

Then St. James presented himself as an Indian knight, and, entering the army of the Shah, won such renown by his heroic deeds, that he was soon raised to the highest posts of honour.

Now, there came from the far east two sovereigns, claiming the hand of the fair Celestine; but she, thinking only of St. James, refused to entertain their proposals.

At a great tournament given in their honour, they both, clothed in glittering armour, entered the lists; so did the seeming Moorish knight. What was the surprise of the King and all his courtiers to behold him overthrow them both! Then he rode up beneath the pavilion of the Princess Celestine, and exhibited to her a ring which she had long before given him. By this she knew that he was her own true knight. He soon found means to tell her of his love, and all that had happened, while Pedrillo did not forget to put in a word in his own favour with her maiden.

They agreed that very night to fly to Spain. Pedrillo, who was cunning in devices, turned their horses' shoes backwards, and thus, when they were seeking safety in the west, it appeared as if they were flying towards the east. Thus evading pursuit, they galloped on, crossed the Red Sea, and, travelling through Africa, the whole party arrived safely in that wondrous town of Seville, in Spain, where St. James was born, and which justly holds itself, in consequence, in the very highest estimation.

CHAPTER VII

THE adventures of the great St. Anthony of
Italy, after he parted from his friends at the brazen
pillar, are now to be described. Taking ship, like
Father Æneas of old, he and his attendant Squire
traversed the Mediterranean Sea, only he sailed
eastward, while the pious Æneas sailed westward,
over it. Numberless were the adventures he
encountered.

Now his ship was tossed by storms, now pursued
by a huge sea monster, with jaws so wide that the
affrighted mariners believed that it was about to
swallow up bodily both them and their ship ; but
St. Anthony, putting on his armour, and standing
on the poop, brandished his spear so manfully in
the monster's face that he effectually kept him at
bay. His faithful Squire shouted also with such
good effect, that the monster was fain to turn tail
and to leave the ship and its honoured freight to
proceed unmolested.

At length Asia's ancient shores were reached,
and travelling on, performing every day unheard-of
wonders, combating with terrible monsters, and
destroying wild beasts innumerable, he and Niccolo
arrived at the far-famed kingdom of Georgia.
They wandered on till they began to ascend, amid
narrow defiles and dark gorges, the rugged ranges
of the mighty Caucasus, high above which Elborus
towers with gigantic splendour. As they climbed
upwards, higher and higher, there appeared before
them a marble castle with gates of brass, which they
guessed, from inquiries they had made, belonged to

the giant Blanderon. Over the principal gate were
these verses :—

" Within this castle lives the scourge of kings ;
A furious giant, whose unconquer'd power
The Georgian monarch in subjection brings,
And keeps his daughters prisoners in his tower:
Seven damsels fair this monstrous giant keeps,
That sing him music while he nightly sleeps.

His sword of steel a thousand knights have felt,
Who for these maidens' sakes have lost their lives ;
Yet, though on many knights he hath death dealt,
This most inhuman giant still survives.
Let simple passengers take heed in time,
When up this mountain height they thoughtless climb.

But knights of worth, and men of noble mind,
If any chance to travel by this tower,
That for these maidens' sake will be so kind
To try their strength against the giant's power,
Shall have a maiden's prayer, both day and night,
To prosper them with good successful fight."

These lines were placed there by the power of
the good fairy of Asia, and were unseen by the
Giant, or he would not, it is presumed, have allowed
them to remain. They so encouraged the valiant
Knight, that, resolving to liberate the ladies, he struck
so mighty a blow on the gate of the castle, with the
pommel of his sword, that it sounded like a clap of
the loudest thunder.

On hearing it, Blanderon, who had been asleep,
started up, and came forth to the gate with a huge
oak-tree in his hand, which he flourished about his
head as if it had been a light battle-axe, in a loud
voice comparing the Knight's spear to a bull-rush,
and threatening to hurl him and his Squire down the
side of the mountain.

"Words without deeds are mere empty things,"
retorted the Knight. "Try what you can do."
And giving his steed to his Squire to hold, he drew
his trusty falchion, and stood ready to receive the
onslaught of his huge antagonist. Blanderon, however, flourished his oak so furiously that St. Anthony
had to jump here and there with the greatest
activity to avoid his strokes.

Now the very earth seemed to shake; now the
castle walls resounded with the blows. The Knight
relaxed not a moment in his efforts, for he saw that
the Giant was stout; and as the sun's heat was very
great, he panted more and more till the moisture
from his brows ran down into his eyes, and almost
blinded him. Observing this, the Knight plied him
with his battle-axe more vigorously than before, till
he was compelled to seek for safety within his castle
walls; but ere he reached them he let fall from his
grasp his huge oak-tree; on which St. Anthony,
redoubling his efforts, smote him so fiercely, that he
sunk down on his knees, unable to fly further
Still undaunted, the Giant drew a dagger twice the
size of any ordinary two-handed sword. With
this he struck right and left so rapidly that the
Knight had hard work indeed to escape its blows,
and still greater to discover a spot in his huge body
in which he might plant a deadly one in return.

At length, however, the Giant grew weary, and
St. Anthony, springing forward, with one stroke
clove his hideous head almost in twain. Then, with
another blow he cut it off, and handed it to Niccolo,
to be carried before him as a trophy of his prowess.
So violent, however, had been the efforts of the
Knight that he also sank fainting on the ground,

when his faithful Squire, believing him to be dead, knelt by his side, and, weeping, mourned bitterly his loss.

Now, it happened that the lovely Rosalinde, one of the daughters of the King of Georgia, who had been taken captive by the Giant, looked over the battlements, and seeing his headless trunk guessed that he had been slain by some gallant knight, and that the end of her servitude had arrived.

Descending to the gate, she beheld the seeming lifeless body of the Champion, and, kneeling opposite to Niccolo, joined her salt tears with his in mourning the fate of so brave a Knight. Then, remembering that there were some precious balms within the castle, she went and fetched them; and having applied them to the limbs of the Champion, their effect was so great that he instantly revived, and sitting up gazed at her with admiration, and inquired who she was. They entreated him to wait till he had been fed and rested within the castle.

While the faithful Niccolo watched by his master's couch, as he slept, the lady Rosalinde was preparing delicates for his repast.

He at length awoke, restored to health and strength; and then, by the lady's advice, he ordered Niccolo to drag the Giant's carcass down upon a craggy rock, to be devoured by hungry ravens; which being done, the Georgian maiden exhibited to him the wonders of the castle. First she conducted him to a brazen tower where were a hundred corselets and other martial furniture of the knights slain by the Giant. Then she conducted him to the stables, where were a hundred steeds, thin and jaded, which they had once be-

strode.   There was also the Giant's bed of iron,
with a covering of carved brass, and with curtains
of leaves of gold.   After this she pointed out to
him a pond of crystal water, on which swam six
milk-white swans, with crowns of gold upon their
heads.

"Know, brave Champion, that these six swans
are my sisters," she observed.   "We all seven are
the daughters of the King of Georgia.   As we
were out hunting one day the Giant from the
battlements of his castle espied us, and, rushing
down, bore us off under his arms before any one
could come to our rescue.   My sisters, by the
power of a kind fairy who had attended at their
birth, were transformed into swans, that they might
escape the tyranny of the Giant, though she was
unable to release them altogether.   I, the eldest,
retained my natural form ;   for, from my skill in
music, I could always quell his anger and tame him
into subjection.   Though I might perchance have
escaped, I remained, in hope some day of liberating
my sisters.   Now, if the good fairy can be found,
we may tell her of the Giant's death, and bring her
hither to restore them to their natural shapes."

"Most lovely lady, we will fly at once to your
father's capital, and send the fairy hither to perform
her grateful task," exclaimed the Knight, placing
the hand of the Princess in his own.   So, taking
the keys of the castle, which were ot wonderous
weight, they locked up the gates, and mounting
their steeds, followed by Niccolo with the Giant's
gory head, they proceeded to the Georgian Court.

On reaching the gate of the city they heard a
peal of bells solemnly tolling forth a funeral knell

On inquiring the cause of this, the aged porter replied :—

"The bells toll for the King's seven daughters. There are seven bells, each one called after the name of a Princess, which never have ceased this doleful melody since the loss of the unhappy ladies, nor ever will till they return."

"Then their tasks are finished," answered the noble-minded Rosalinde. "We bring you tidings of the Princesses."

Whereat the aged porter, ravished with joy, ran to the steeple and stopped the bells. Hearing the bells cease their wonted mournful melody, up started the King of Georgia, and hastened to the gate to inquire the cause. There, to his joy, he beheld his long-lost daughter in company with a strange knight and attendant squire. Hearing the wonderful tale, he commanded all his courtiers to put on the lugubrious weeds of mourning, and to accompany him to the castle of the Giant, that there perchance he might discover some means of releasing his six other daughters, while the noble-minded Rosalinde and St. Anthony were left to take care of the city till his return.

When the King of Georgia, after long delay, did not return, the Italian Knight declared, in impassioned words, that he must proceed in search of those adventures for the sake of which he had left his native land. To this the noble-minded Rosalinde replied :—

"Oh! most princely-minded Champion of Italy! It is not Georgia can harbour me when thou art absent. The sky shall be no sky, the sea no sea, the earth no earth, if thou do prove inconstant ; but if you will not take me with you, these tender hands of mine shall hang upon your horse's bridle, till my body, like Theseus's son, be dashed against the hard flint stones ; yet, hard as they are, not harder than I shall deem your heart."

One only reply to this appeal could the princely-minded Champion make. It was to tell her that he would bear her away forthwith as his own true bride. And they thus both being agreed, habited as a page in green sarcenet, her buskins of the smoothest kid-skin, and her rapier of Lydian steel, secured over her shoulder by an orange-coloured scarf, and mounted on a gentle palfrey, she quitted the land of Georgia ; one of her maidens, habited also in page's guise, attending, whom Niccolo took under his especial care. Thus they travelled ; he the bravest, boldest knight that ever wandered by the way, and she the loveliest lady that ever mortal eye beheld.

CHAPTER VIII

AND now the adventures of the far-famed St. Andrew of Scotland claim our attention, after he quitted the brazen pillar, followed by his faithful Squire, Murdoch M'Alpine of that ilk. On he travelled eastward, in the face of the rays of the glittering sun, which sparkled on his shield and casque with dazzling brightness, and so astonished all beholders that they fled dismayed before him, till he crossed the wild territories of Russia, and entered the wilder deserts of Siberia. Then, turning north, he found himself in a region where, for many weary months, the sun never rose, and he and the faithful Murdoch had to discover their way by poking before them with their spears, every moment expecting to meet with some huge monster with whom they might be called to combat. Nor did they expect in vain, for suddenly a loud growl assailed their ears, and the moon, just then rising, exhibited to them a whole army of bears, prepared to dispute their onward progress.

"Draw your broad-sword, mon, and follow me," cried St. Andrew, shaking his spear.

The Squire, tucking up his plaid carefully, that it might not be torn or soiled, with loud shouts obeyed, and soon both were dashing and slashing away among the infuriated brutes. The heads of numbers rolled upon the snow, which for miles round was ensanguined with their blood.

"Few creatures are more difficult to get rid of than bears," observed the Knight, charging again. "On, Murdoch, on, we'll do it if it is to be done, for what men dare they can do!"

Thus shouting and slaying, the Knight and his Squire fought on for many hours, till the survivors of the bears, discovering that they were likely to get the worst of it in the end, took to flight, and stopped not till they reached the North Pole, where they stopped only because they could go no further, and where St. Andrew agreed that it was not worth while following them.

His next encounter was with a nation of people with heads like foxes, from whose cunning arts and guiles he had the greatest difficulty in escaping. Although conquered by the power of his arms, they still appeared with fresh tricks to entrap him. When, at length, he had fought his way out from among them, he found himself in a dismal vale, the air still dark as Erebus, where he heard the blowing of unseen furnaces, the boiling of cauldrons, the rattling of armour, the trampling of horses, the jingling of chains, the roaring of wild beasts, the hissing of serpents, and the cries of unearthly spirits, and such like dreadful sounds, which would have made any other hearts than those of St. Andrew of Scotland, and of his faithful squire, Murdoch M'Alpine of that ilk, quake and tremble with fear; but passing calmly amid them, and undergoing hardships incredible, under which knights and squires, born in more southern climes, would have sunk exhausted, they arrived in the kingdom of Georgia, nor rested till they reached the foot of the mountain on which stood the castle within whose iron walls the six fair daughters of the King were still held in durance, in the shape of swans, with golden crowns upon their heads.

When the valiant Champion of Scotland beheld the lofty situation of the castle, and the invincible strength it seemed to be of, he suspected some strange adventure to befall him; so, buckling close his armour, which, on account of the heat he had loosened, and drawing his sword, he climbed the mountain, when he espied, on a craggy rock, the headless body of the Giant, on which the ravens and other birds of prey were feeding. Then he approached the castle gate, when, what was his astonishment to see a long procession of mourners come forth, with the King of Georgia at their head; and, on inquiry, was told that the old man mourned for his six daughters, whom he could by no means get changed back into their natural shapes.

St. Andrew, on hearing this strange tale, expressed his firm belief, in language somewhat strong, that such things could not be.

Whereon the King and all his courtiers were highly indignant, and numberless knights stepped forth, and challenged the stranger to mortal combat. The lists were quickly prepared. Then the valiant Champion of Christendom entered the arena, when the King, in company with many Georgian lords, was present to behold the contest. Thrice had St. Andrew traced his war-steed up and down the lists, flourishing his lance, at the top whereof hung a pendant of gold, on which, in silver letters, was traced, "This day a martyr or a conqueror!" Whereon there entered a knight in exceeding bright armour, mounted on a courser as white as snow, whose caparison was the colour of the elements.

A fierce encounter followed; but the Georgian was defeated, and retired in disgrace from the lists.

Then entered a knight in green armour, his steed an iron grey. Loud rang their spears against their shields, fierce clashed their swords, and clanged their battle-axes, till the Georgian warrior fairly took to flight.

The third knight who entered wore a black corselet, and his huge war-horse was covered with a veil of sable silk. In his hand he bore a baton of mighty weight, and bound round with iron; but no sooner did the champions meet than their lances shivered in pieces from the furious shock, and flew high up into the air, when, alighting from their steeds, they resumed the combat with their keen-edged falchions, the sparks flying from their helmets as from a blacksmith's anvil.

The faithful Murdoch meantime looked on with anxious gaze, when he was accosted by a little old woman of mean aspect, who had in vain tried to obtain information from the other bystanders.

"Why is it you want to know, Mother?" he asked, careful not to give a hurried answer, though he bowed politely.

The old woman, who was in reality a good fairy, replied, " Because I have come here to do some good ; but while a scene of mortal strife is taking place I cannot employ my power."

Then Murdoch told her all he knew about the matter ; whereon she advised him to hurry to his master when the present combat should be over, and to bid him declare his belief that the account was true, and to offer to bring the Princesses forth in their proper shapes.

Meantime the combat between the Scottish Champion and the Black Knight continued with unabated fury. Any advantage gained by one was foiled by the other, till at length St. Andrew, uttering his battle-cry, struck so mighty a blow with his battle-axe, that he clave the Georgian's burgonet, and his head beneath, from his crown to his shoulders, and his body fell lifeless on the ground.

This so enraged the King that he would have ordered the Scottish Knight to have been slain, when Murdoch rushed forward and gave the fairy's message.

The Champion spoke as she had directed, when the King, who was of a placable disposition, though somewhat hasty, consented to his request.

"Swear, most noble King, upon my sword, that you will not attempt any foul treachery to me or my follower, on account of the Champion I have slain, until I have accomplished the task I have now undertaken."

On this the old King, descending from his throne, bent over the gallant St. Andrew's sword, and swore as he desired.

The Knight entered the castle, and repaired to the garden, when, instead of finding an ugly old woman, he beheld a lady of radiant beauty, for such was indeed the Fairy.

"You see yonder six swans," said she; "as they approach strike boldly with your sword six strokes, nor fear the consequences."

The Knight stood by the side of the crystal lake, and as he stood, his glittering falchion in his hand, the six swans swam gracefully up. Six times he struck, and each time the head of one of the swans flew up; but in its stead appeared, wonderful to relate, a beautiful maiden, whom the Knight handed with true courtesy off her liquid pedestal on to dry land. Thus, in a few minutes, the Champion was surrounded by six of the most lovely damsels the world ever saw, habited in green hunting-suits, each almost equal to Diana herself, going forth armed for the chase.

"You have done well, noble Champion," said the Fairy. "You did not despise me, or my words, when I appeared old and ugly, and from henceforth you will find me ever ready to aid and protect you, as you travel on in search of those heroic adventures after which your heart pants. I bid you farewell; though, remember, that I will come when you sum-mon me;" saying this the Fairy mounted a golden chariot drawn by peacocks, and, rapidly gliding

through the air, disappeared amid the clouds which
floated round the sides of that lofty mountain.
Scarcely had she gone, and the six ladies were
pouring forth their thanks to the noble Knight who
had delivered them from their cruel bondage, when
the King of Georgia, followed by all his knights
and courtiers, entered the garden of the castle to
ascertain what had become of the strange Knight.

Nothing could exceed his astonishment, and
delight, and gratitude, when St. Andrew presented
to him his six daughters in their proper forms.
"You deserve them all," exclaimed the Monarch,
in the warmth of his emotion. To which the
Scottish Knight, with true modesty, replied, that he
considered one far more than he deserved, and that
as yet he felt inclined to remain a bachelor.

The next day, after a sumptuous banquet which
the King's cooks prepared in the Giant's castle, the
whole party marched back to the palace of the
Georgian Monarch with banners streaming, cymbals
clashing, and drums and trumpets sounding joyful
melody. When, however, sad to relate, the King
inquired for his eldest daughter, he found that she
had fled away with the Champion of Italy.

This event, so grievous to the heart of the King,
made him defer all the triumphant arrangements
which were forming to do honour to the Scottish
Knight and to his six fair daughters.

When, also, St. Andrew heard that one of his
noble comrades was so near at hand, calling Murdoch
to his side, he bade him prepare for their departure.
Wishing to avoid the pain of parting with the six
Princesses, and, lest their honoured sire might renew
his generous offer, St. Andrew, without bidding

farewell to the King of Georgia, or to his chief councillors and ministers of state, and other great lords of the realm, set off from the capital in pursuit of St. Anthony of Italy and the fair Rosalinde.

The next day, when the six Princesses heard of the departure of the Knight they so much admired, providing themselves with sufficient treasure and habiliments suited for travelling, they left by stealth their father's palace, mounted on six white palfreys, and attended by six maidens on asses, intending to find out the victorious and renowned Champion of Scotland, or to end their lives in single blessedness in some pious retirement in a foreign land.

No sooner did the news of his daughters' flight reach the King of Georgia, than attiring himself in homely russet, like a pilgrim, with an ebony staff in his hand, tipped with silver, he took his departure, all alone, from his palace, resolved to recover his beloved children, or to lay his bones to rest in some unknown spot, where, forgotten, he might rest at peace.

When his councillors, ministers of state, and other great lords heard of his sudden and secret departure, grief intolerable struck their hearts, the palace gates were covered with sable cloth, all pleasures were at an end, and ladies and courtly dames sat sighing in their chambers; where, for the present, we will leave them to speak of other themes.

CHAPTER IX

THE noble, illustrious, and wonderful deeds of St. Patrick, the far-famed and renowned Champion of Old Ireland, that gem of the ocean, are now to be recounted—not forgetting those of his faithful and attached squire, Terence O'Grady; though of the latter many less partial histories are somewhat unaccountably silent.

After they quitted the brazen pillar, they, too, traversed that sea so famed in ancient story. But their ship being wrecked as they were approaching the land, and sinking beneath their feet, they mounted on the backs of two huge dolphins, which were swimming by at the time, and which St. Patrick caught with cunningly-devised hooks; and thus towing their steeds, they reached in safety the sandy shores of Africa. There landing, while they sat by the sea-side burnishing their arms, which were slightly rusty from the salt air, the sweetest strains of music struck upon their ears. The Squire listened, and rising from the rock on which he sat, he wandered on to discover whence they proceeded.

What was his astonishment, as he looked into a cavern half filled with water, to behold a dozen lovely nymphs, almost immersed in the crystal sea, combing their golden locks, while from their throats came forth those warbling sounds.

The Squire gazed enravished. " Och, but you are beautiful creatures! " he exclaimed, forgetting that his voice might be heard. The maidens started, like frightened deer, at the sound; and then, seeing the faithful Terence as he looked over the rock, they swam towards him, putting out their arms, and endeavouring to grasp his hands. A more prudent person would have withdrawn, and suspected treachery; but such an idea never occurred to the mind of the warm-hearted Irishman.

" A pleasant morning to ye, my pretty damsels! "

quoth he, offering his hand to the first who came up, expecting to assist her to land; for, as they were dressed in sea-green garments, and had wreaths of red and white coral on their heads, he thought that they would have no objection to come out of the water. Instead, however, of coming out themselves, the first held him tight, and others arriving caught hold of him likewise, and began to pull and pull away till the faithful Terence discovered, without a doubt, that it was their purpose to pull him in.

"But I can't swim, Ladies!" he exclaimed. "I shall spoil my armour and wet my clothes—let me go, if you please, now." He wished to speak them fair, though doubts as to what they were began to rise up in his mind. "Och, now, let me go, I say! A joke's a joke all the world over; but if you souse me head over ears in that pool, and drown me entirely, it will be a very bad one to my taste now." The more, however, he shouted and struggled the harder the damsels pulled.

Though Terence was a stout fellow, and had been in many a hot fight in foreign lands, and not a few scrimmages in Old Ireland, he never had had such a struggle in his life. At last his cries brought St. Patrick to his aid, (for who would the Champion of Ireland have helped more willingly than Terence O'Grady?), and seizing the other arm, he hauled away lustily against the twelve sea-nymphs, whom he at once discovered to be mermaids, who had set their hearts on carrying off his faithful Squire to their coral homes beneath the waves.

Between the mermaids on one side, and his master on the other, hauling away with all their might, poor Terence was very nearly torn in pieces. Still he struggled and strove, entreating his master not to let him go.

Shouts of merry laughter issued from the throats of the mermaids; but though they diverted themselves with the terror of the faithful Terence, they did not cease to pull at him the less hard, till he began to fear that, if they could not have the whole, they would have a bit of him to a certainty.

St. Patrick himself saw full well that the matter was no joke; but how to rescue his Squire without using his sword, and against that all his knightly feelings revolted, even he was sorely puzzled to discover.

As it happened, there dwelt not far off, in a lofty castle of iron walls and golden battlements, a monstrous giant, who had long sought one of these mermaids in marriage; but she fearing his temper, and not wishing to leave her watery home, had ever disdainfully refused to listen to his proposals. He now was wandering along the shore in search of her to prosecute his suit.

As he looked down into the cave and saw the mermaids, one of whom was his beloved, pulling away on one side at the faithful Terence, while St. Patrick pulled on the other, he uttered a loud roar of rage and fury. The sound so alarmed the mermaids that they let go their hold, and fled away in terror, to hide themselves in their coral homes, while St. Patrick, looking up, beheld the Giant frowning down defiance at him.

The Irish Champion, nothing daunted, drew his falchion. "Ah, my trusty weapon, thou hast at length found a worthy enemy!" he exclaimed,

climbing up the cliff towards the Giant, closely
followed by the faithful Terence. Black as jet was
the Giant, but blacker were his looks, yet blackest
of all were his intentions. Behind him stood a
huge crocodile, opening wide its immense jaws, and
threatening to devour any one who came within their
compass. Many a stout warrior would have avoided
the encounter; but St. Patrick boldly advanced,
trusting in a good cause, his own arm, and his well-
tempered sword, feeling assured, also, that Terence
would give a good account of the crocodile.

Quickly were heard to sound the ringing strokes
of the Champion's trusty falchion against the black
shield of the Giant, whose huge battle-axe dealt
many a fearful blow in return. Fiercely raged the
combat. Blow after blow was given and taken with
right good will, while the Giant bellowed out so
loudly his threats of vengeance against the valiant
Knight, that the rocks and distant mountains
resounded with his cries mingled with the clang
of desperate strife.

Terence stood by to watch the contest, not to
deprive his loved master of a shred of glory, till he
saw the crocodile opening his monstrous jaws to
snap at his legs. Then he saw that the time for
action had arrived, and, rushing up, began to assail
the brute with right good will.

The crocodile snapped and snapped his huge jaws
with a sound which made the hills ring and ring
again; but he failed to get the faithful Terence
within the power of his grinders; at the same time,
in vain the Squire sought a vulnerable point into
which to thrust his trusty sword. The length of
the monster's snout prevented him from reaching his

eyes, and, as to getting a fair thrust at his shoulders, that seemed utterly impossible.

All this time St. Patrick and the Giant, it must not be forgotten, were fighting furiously.

" Let my tame crocodile alone, or I'll make mincemeat of you when I have killed your master ! " cried the Giant hoarsely, through his clinched teeth.

" Faith, then, I hope that time will never arrive then, my beauty," answered the faithful Terence, making a spring, and leaping nimbly on the crocodile's back. " It's not exactly the sort of steed I'd choose, except for the honour of riding, but I'll make him pay the piper, at all events ; " whereupon he began slashing away with his trusty sword most furiously on the neck and shoulders of the crocodile. A delicate maiden might as well have tried to pierce the hide of an aged hippopotamus with a bodkin.

At last, losing patience, he sprang to his feet on the back of the monster, and plunged his sword into one of his eyes, just as he was about to make a snap at St. Patrick's thigh. The crocodile, feeling itself wounded, turned aside, when the Squire plunged his weapon into the other eye.

Thus blinded, and furious with pain, the brute rushed forward, snapping in every direction, and running against his master, caught hold of the calf of his leg with a gripe so firm that the Giant, groaning with pain, turned aside his proud looks to see what was the matter.

The opportunity was not lost on St. Patrick, who, pressing forward, plunged his falchion into the neck of his antagonist, who, bellowing louder than ten thousand bulls, made a desperate cut with his battle-

axe at the helm of the Knight. The Champion
sprang aside, and the blow descended on the neck
of the tame crocodile, whereby its head was severed
from its body, Terence narrowly escaping from the
effects of the blow.

The death of his favourite brute enraged the
Giant still further ; but rage invariably blinds
judgment, and neglecting his proper guards, he soon
found himself treated as he had treated the crocodile, his head, by a stroke of the Knight's battle-axe,
falling on the sand, while his eyes continued to roll
most horribly, as if still animated with fury and
malicious hatred.

The faithful Terence having found a huge brazen
key, and a purse of gold, in the Giant's pocket, and
transferred the latter to his own, to be ready for
future emergencies, St. Patrick and he left the two
carcasses to be devoured by the birds of the air,
and proceeded to the Giant's castle. The huge
brazen key opened the castle gate ; when entering,
they wandered amazed through the spacious halls,
and courts, and galleries, admiring the wonders
there collected. In the armoury were numerous
tall and straight trees of cocoa-nut and pine, with
iron or steel points, which served the Giant as
spears ; his sword even St. Patrick could scarecly
lift, while near was another tree, taller than all the
rest, with a cable at one end, and a hook bigger
than a huge ship's anchor, with which in his hand
the Giant sat on a rock and bobbed for whales.

In the stables, instead of some vast horses,
which they expected to find, capable of carrying so
monstrous a being, they beheld rows of alligators
and hippopotami, which the Giant was wont to

harness to his brazen chariots when he went to war, or out a pleasuring; while, as no saddles or bridles were found, it was evident that he possessed no steed capable of bearing his ponderous weight.

St. Patrick and his Squire, making themselves at home in the Giant's castle, passed several pleasant days, while they recovered from the fatigues of their combat and refreshed themselves after their voyage. Then, that they might keep their own steeds ready for any emergency, they harnessed a dozen hippopotami, and as many tame crocodiles, to one of the Giant's chariots, and so, with great comfort and convenience, proceeded on their journey. The canopy of the chariot was of azure silk fringed with silver, which sheltered them from the warm rays of the sun.

" Faith, this is pleasanter far than riding along over a dusty road! " quoth the Squire to the Knight, with that easy familiarity which the superior delighted to encourage in his faithful attendant. " What would they say in Old Ireland if they saw us two now a travelling along, quite at our ease, over the burning plains of Africa! " Whereat St. Patrick made some suitable reply. But their pleasant conversation was cut short by the sounds of some terrible wails and laments, uttered by female voices, and at the same time of loud harsh voices and rude laughter, proceeding from out of a neighbouring wood, which they beheld before them. On this Terence whipped on the crocodiles and hippopotami with right good will, their own trusty steeds trotting behind till they arrived at the borders of the wood; when, securely fastening their chariot to a stout tree, they mounted their chargers, and dashed forward, in the direction from whence the cries proceeded.

Louder and louder grew the shrieks and lamentations, till the Knight and his Squire arrived at a spot whence, looking down into a sylvan dell, they beheld a sight which made their hearts melt with pity, and their blood run cold with horror. There, with the salt tears running down their cheeks, and their eyes imploring mercy and pity, they saw six lovely damsels, clad in green garments, bound to as many trees, while round them danced a hundred fierce satyrs, terrible of aspect, and hideous to behold.

Each satyr was armed with a huge club of the size of a tree, which he flourished wildly, and on his other arm he bore a shield of vast proportions, like the moon at the full, as she rises over the housetops; while scabbardless two-handed swords hung with brazen chains by their sides, and long-bows and quivers full of arrows were suspended at their backs; their voices as they danced giving forth those hideous sounds which had attracted the Knight and Squire.

Near the ladies stood six milk-white palfreys, and a little way behind, who had not at first been seen, six other damsels, their dress and bearing showing them to be the serving maidens of the lovely ladies in green. In an instant the heart of the Champion of Ireland, and of his faithful Squire, were all in a flame, burning to rescue these six lovely ladies and their six inestimable serving women from the power of those hideous satyrs; so, drawing their falchions, and uttering the war-cry of Old Ireland, they dashed with headlong speed in among them, cutting and slashing and hewing away before any of those terrific beings had any knowledge of their approach.

Soon recovering themselves, after a few of their
number had bitten the dust, the hideous satyrs,
uniting in one body, and seeing that their enemies
consisted but of a single knight and his squire,
flourished their huge clubs, and with loud shouts,
louder than the roaring of ten thousand bulls,
advanced towards them.

Heroically fought St. Patrick, and manfully
combated his Squire. The blows from the monstrous clubs of the hideous satyrs fell like hail about
their helmets; but their thirsty swords rapidly
drank the life-blood of their foes, and now one
satyr, now another, was overthrown. Still more
came on. Some stood at a distance, shooting their
arrows from their long-bows; others came around,
with their two-handed swords, and struck and
slashed so fiercely that it required all the activity
and courage of both Knight and Squire, of which
they fortunately possessed so large a portion, to keep
their enemies at bay. Still the sight of the lovely
ladies tied to the trees, not forgetting the six serving
maidens, as well as their own honour, and desire for
glory and renown, induced them to persevere.

Full one-third of the hideous satyrs had sunk
lifeless from their stalwart blows, while many others
limped off sorely wounded and maimed; yet the
remainder, with a perseverance worthy of a better
cause, fiercely continued the combat.

At length, St. Patrick telling Terence to escape,
wheeled his horse round as if to fly, but it was only
a cunning device, as his faithful Squire well knew;
for, instantly returning to the charge with redoubled
vigour among the scattered ranks of his foes, he
dealt such slaughter and destruction among them,

that the survivors were fain to fly far away, howling, into the distant woods, which resounded with their mournful cries, leaving the six ladies and their six serving maidens to the care and protection of the gallant Knight and his attendant.

While St. Patrick cut loose the cords from the fair limbs of the six ladies all clothed in green, Terence performed the same office for the serving maidens.

After they had been refreshed by some pure draughts from the neighbouring crystal brook, and partaken of such fare as the Champion could offer them, he led them forth from the wood, and with courteous attentions, and many polite expressions, placed them in his chariot drawn by the crocodiles and hippopotami. Then, and not till then, did he inquire their names, and state, and nation.

The eldest replied :—" Know, most puissant and valiant Knight, that we are the unfortunate daughters of the King of Georgia. Our lives since our births have been unhappy. First, we were carried off by a monstrous giant, and, being turned into swans for seven long years, lost sight of the outer world, neither knowing what dresses were worn, how fashions were changed, and many other important matters.

" At length, through the courage of a noble Knight, St. Andrew of Scotland, of whom you have doubtless heard, we were happily released from our thraldom. What, however, was our astonishment when we got back to our father's court to find that our eldest sister had departed as the bride of another famed Champion, St. Anthony of Italy, by whose mighty prowess the giant had been slain ;

and in a brief time St. Andrew, hearing of this, also set off in search of his former comrade and brother knight.

"Now—why need we be ashamed to confess it? —we had allowed a feeling of regard to spring up in our bosoms for that worthy Knight, and we all agreed that we could no longer exist out of his society; and so we also set off from our father's court, resolved to search for him the world around, and bring him back to our native land, or lie down, and mournful die beside his tomb."

"The noble Champion for whom you took in hand this weary travel is my much approved good friend," exclaimed St. Patrick. "To get a sight of him I would go more miles than there are trees throughout this mighty continent; therefore, will my faithful squire, Terence O'Grady, whom I now crave leave to make known unto you, and I travel in your company, and in that of your six serving maidens, till we have found the right noble St. Andrew, or some other of those six brave Knights of Christendom who for seven summers I have not seen."

Much pleased with the discourse and the polished courtesy of St. Patrick, the six princesses consented to his proposal; and thus we will, for the present, leave them journeying in the giant's chariot, drawn by the dozen crocodiles and hippopotami, and followed by the six maidens and their six milk-white palfreys, and escorted on either side by St. Patrick and his faithful Squire, in the direction they believed St. Andrew had taken.

CHAPTER X

THE last but not the least of all the Seven
Champions to be mentioned famed for heroic
courage and gallantry is that most noble and
renowned Knight, St. David of Wales. After
he had quitted the brazen pillar, followed by his
faithful attendant, Owen ap Rice, he proceeded
towards the up-rising of the sun, visiting many of
the courts of the first monarchs of Europe, attending many tournaments, engaging in many desperate
battles, and performing innumerable heroic deeds;
which his faithful Squire took very great care to
recount, nor did he allow his histories to lose anything in the telling. Wonderful indeed were the
numbers of foes his master's sword had slain; huge
were the giants he had overthrown; savage were
the wild beasts he had slaughtered; terrific were the
monsters he had put to flight; powerful were the
magicians whose guiles he had circumvented; and
horrible were the spirits, and ghosts, and goblins amid
whom he had fought his onward way; indeed few
could hear the faithful Owen recount his master's
deeds, and eke his own, without being impressed
with the belief that more heroic Knight did not
exist, nor more brave and trusty Squire.

Thus they journeyed on till Europe was left
behind; and entering the ancient continent of Asia,
they arrived at the court of the far-famed Emperor
of Tartary. Here St. David's fame had preceded
him, and they were received with all that courtesy
which to so valiant a Knight was due.

On the day of their arrival a sumptuous entertainment was prepared, at which all the chief lords and nobles of the realm were present, when huge beakers of rosy wine were quaffed ; nor could any one compete with St. David in the quantity of the generous liquor he imbibed. For the following day a grand tournament was arranged, when it was expected that the noblest feats of arms ever beheld in the empire would be performed.

From far and near came valiant knights from all the neighbouring provinces, habited in every conceivable style of richest armour ; yet none surpassed St. David in the sumptuousness of his plume and burgonet, the trappings of his steed, the richness of his scarf, the splendour of his shield and breastplate, or of his whole armour, which, from his lofty helm to his knightly spurs, shone with resplendent beauty. Numerous champions entered the lists, and many desperate encounters took place. At length St. David rode in, followed by the faithful Owen carrying his spear. The trumpets sounded, St. David took his spear, and shaking it aloft prepared for the encounter. A Knight, one of the chief nobles of Tartary, was his first opponent. Of blue steel was his casque, and armour, and mighty shield, while a blue scarf floated from his shoulders. Bravely the Tartar Knight bore himself, and bravely he withstood the terrible shock of St. David's lance. A second time the two Knights charged, when St. David, mustering all his powers, struck the Tartar a blow so terrible that he sent him reeling from his saddle, and with a hollow groan he fell senseless on the ground ; but time will not permit an account of each separate combat of that far-famed tournament.

Six valiant Knights did St. David meet, each of whom was vanquished by his arm. At length, the only son and heir of the Emperor, seeing that no more worthy antagonist could be found, and willing to retrieve the disgrace he conceived his countrymen had received, entered the lists, and bravely challenged the Champion of Wales. The heart of the gallant St. David bounded at the thought of engaging in so noble a contest as that with the Emperor's son, and he declared himself ready to commence the course whenever it was the pleasure of the noble prince to meet his lance.

" No time like the present, Sir Knight," replied the gallant Tartar, who was arrayed in armour of rare and curious workmanship, studded all over with gold and precious gems.

" It were a pity to slay so brave a prince," thought St. David; " yet for the honour of my country, than which no nobler exists, as also for my own, than whom no * * * " (what St. David thought need not be repeated). " If he presses me it must be done."

The trumpets sounded, the steeds sprang forward, the ground trembled beneath their feet, clouds of dust arose in the air ; terrific was the shock, but both Knights kept their seats, though both were sorely pressed. Again they charged, with a like result. A third time they met, and St. David felt that he was reeling in his saddle ; but recovering himself by a mighty effort, he prepared for another and more desperate encounter. Little wotted the proud son of the great Emperor of all the Tartars with what a doughty Champion he had to contend ; little thought he of the gallant heroes that far-distant

land of Cambria was able to produce. Shaking his
spear, he shouted loudly to St. David to prepare
himself for an overthrow. The Welsh Knight only
grasped his own spear the tighter in consequence,
and pressed his knees the firmer against his charger's
sides.

"And the Prince expects that he is going to
throw my master, does he?" observed the faithful
Owen. "Let him beware of St. David; I may
tell him he has borne down to the ground twelve as
good men as he is, with one thrust of his lance,
before now."

The trumpets sounded, and the Tartar Prince
and the Champion of Wales met in the middle of
the lists. Terrific was the encounter; the spear of
the Tartar Prince was shivered into a thousand
fragments; but the Welsh Knight, with true
gallantry, let his fall by his side, and grasped his
battle-axe, that they might fight on equal terms.
Already, however, had the spear inflicted a desperate
wound on the Prince's side; but his pride would
not let him yield. Now sparks of fire flew thickly
around them from the extraordinary rapidity of their
strokes, so that they appeared to be fighting in the
midst of a furnace (so Owen the faithful Squire
ever afterwards averred), till at length St. David's
axe descended with force so terrific on the helm of
the Tartar Prince that he clove it in two, nor did
the cruel weapon stop till it had pierced the brain of
the hapless heir to the throne of the great Emperor
of Tartary.

When the spectators beheld what had occurred,
loud cries of grief, anger, and dismay rent the air;
the great Emperor and all his courtiers, from the

highest to the lowest, crying louder than any one else. The lists were immediately broken up, and the Emperor, ordering the Welsh Knight to be brought before him, retired into his palace. The obsequies of that precious jewel of Tartary, now dimmed by death, being concluded, the Emperor, having ceased his woeful lamentations and sad sighs, thus addressed the Welsh Champion :—

" Know that there dwells on the borders of Tartary a mighty Magician, Ormandine by name, who holds an enchanted castle and garden, within the magic walls of which whoever enters never again returns. Now truly, although thou deservest death for what thou hast done, yet if thou wilt adventure into the Magician's domains, and bring hither his head, I grant thee not only life, but therewithal the crown of Tartary after my death."

This strange adventure highly pleased the noble Champion of Wales, and he expressed himself ready forthwith to depart about it. On which the Emperor bound him by his oath of knighthood, and by the love he bore his native country, never to follow any other adventure till he had performed the promise he now had given.

In three days he and the faithful Owen, having made all preparation, were ready to set out. Travelling eastward for many a weary day, though conversing pleasantly to beguile the way, they at length reached the confines of a dreadful forest, the trees twisting and twining in every direction, and briers and creepers of all sorts, with long thorns and hooks, hanging from all the branches. Mysterious flames seemed to be bursting forth, wavering and flickering in the dark recesses of the forest, while amid the boughs flew birds of evil omen, night-owls, and ravens, and bats, and other winged things of hideous form, with harsh and croaking voices. Within this forest, so St. David had learned, stood the castle of the Magician Ormandine.

"My faithful Owen," he exclaimed, "by my honour and my oath of knighthood, I am bound to enter and to traverse this strange and woeful wood; but do you wait my return without, and if I never do return, go to my kinsmen, in our native land, and tell them all about my sad and melancholy end."

The faithful Owen, on hearing these words, burst into tears, and replied: "My long-loved honoured Master, if there were ten thousand forests, and if in each thrice ten thousand ill-doing necromancers lived, and if through each you had to fight your way, I would remain steadfast by your side, and fight as long as arm, and hand, and sword could do their work."

"Then onward into this dreadful forest, my faithful Owen, let us go!" exclaimed St. David, drawing his sword, and beginning to hew away at the creepers and briers which impeded their progress. In this labour he was ably seconded by the faithful Owen; and thus, by slow degrees, they worked their onward way. As they proceeded, the shouts and shrieks increased, the sky overhead was filled with lurid meteors, and hideous and ill-omened birds flew thickly around their heads, screeching their terrific notes into the ears of the adventurous strangers.

"Few things worth having can be obtained without difficulty and perseverance," exclaimed St. David, as he went on cutting and cutting away at the creepers. "As to all the hooting, and the screeching, and crying which assail our ears, it cannot hurt us if we take no heed to it. Few noble enterprises have ever been undertaken without numbers of people, like those hideous night-owls, endeavouring to hoot them down."

Thus manfully cutting and hewing away, they at length came in sight of the dark and frowning, damp, and moss-overgrown walls of an ancient castle. Near it was a huge rock, still more damp and moss-covered than the castle-walls. In this rock, by magic art, was enclosed a sword, the hilt being the only part which could be seen. It was of steel work, engraven curiously, and set with jaspers, sapphires, and other precious gems. Around the pommel was engraven, in golden letters, the following words :—

" By magic spells remain most firmly bound,
The world's strange wonder unknown by any one,
Till that a knight within the north be found
To pull the sword from out this rock of stone :
Then end my charms, my magic arts and all,
By whose strong hand sage Ormandine must fall."

"A northern knight !—that must mean me," exclaimed St. David. " Undoubtedly, I am destined to pull the magic sword from out of that rock. See how I'll do it ! " On this, dismounting from his steed, he grasped hold of the hilt, and began to pull and pull away right manfully ; but in vain he pulled, and tugged, and hauled ; not a hundredth part of an inch had he drawn forth of the sword, but, still persevering, he would not let go. At length, the faithful Owen entreated that he might be allowed to come and help. Then Knight and Squire tugged and tugged away, but still the sword

would not move. Next, putting both their hands
to the huge hilt, and their feet against the rock,
they bethought them most surely that they would
move it. Scarcely, however, had they in that guise
begun to pull, than there arose around them fearful
shouts of mocking laughter, and, the gates of the
castle opening wide, twelve hideous dwarfs, with
faces black as coal, and bodies horribly deformed,
issued forth, and bearing in their hands some iron
chains, which clanged as they moved, approached,
with grinning mouths and threatening gestures, the
Knight and his Squire.

St. David and the faithful Owen would fain have
let go the richly gemmed hilt of the magic sword,
but when they strove to do so they found their
hands clinched firmly to it. Now they struggled
as much to free their hands as before they had to
draw out the sword. But in vain was all their
tugging and struggling.

The dwarfs stood round awhile to enjoy their
dismay, and then throwing the iron chains around
them, they bound them in fetters which no earthly
power could undo, and carried them away, helpless
as infants in their nurses' arms, to the magic castle.

There, in the centre of an iron hall of vast
dimensions and sombre hue—the only light emitted
from a lurid torch burning at the further end—on
iron beds, of which a countless number appeared
ranged around, lay writhing the victims which the
fell Magician's cruelty had left bound. There, for
many years, till the full term of seven was accomplished, we, too, will leave them, daily visited by
the Enchanter Ormandine, who came to mock at,
and gloat over their misery.

"Ah! ah!" he exclaimed, with a voice croaking like ten thousand frogs, and loud as thunder, "you came to cut off my head, and carry the gory trophy to the Emperor; but now you find, my friends, you've caught a Tartar."

Notwithstanding, however, this conduct of the Enchanter, his chief captive was not so miserable as he supposed. A kind fairy all the time watched over him; and as St. David lay on his couch she sent four of her attendant spirits, in the form of damsels, of no mean beauty, who tended him with the gentlest care, and brought him fruits and other luxuries, which they offered whenever he awoke, and then sang him to sleep again with their sweet voices, so that his time passed far more agreeably than would certainly otherwise have been the case, or the Enchanter had any idea of.

CHAPTER XI

SEVEN times had frosty-bearded winter covered the ground with snow, and behung the trees with crystal icicles, since the Champion St. George, and the faithful De Fistycuff, lay groaning in their far-off dungeon in Egypt, for having ventured to assert that crocodiles, and apes, and snakes, were not fit objects of reverence.

One day, as by chance the Knight was wringing his hands, in despair of ever getting free, he chanced to rub in a peculiar manner the magic ring which the Fairy Sabrina had given him. A bright light was forthwith emitted from it, which increased and increased till it filled the chamber, and from the midst of it appeared the Fairy herself, in her chariot drawn by ten peacocks.

" Gallant Knight, why did you not summon me before ? " she asked, in her sweet voice ; and St. George had to confess, with shame, that he had forgotten all about the power of the magic ring.

" I cannot free you from this prison by magic power ; but I will give you tools with which you may free yourselves, and then you will set more value on your liberty than if you had gained it without toil. I never afford aid to any who are not ready to labour for themselves."

The Fairy having thus spoken, supplied the Knight and his Squire with hammers, chisels, spades, mattocks, and crowbars.

" Your steeds and weapons you will find ready outside the gates," added the Fairy. " When once more prepared for battle, go forth, and conquer."

The Knight and De Fistycuff felt their strength and spirits wonderfully improved at these words, and already they fancied themselves scouring over the plain in pursuit of a thousand flying foes.

" But is there no gallant achievement, no heroic deed, which you would desire me to perform, as a mark of my gratitude ? " asked St. George, after he had duly thanked the Fairy for the aid she had wrought him.

" Well spoken," answered the Fairy ; " yes, there languishes, even now, a brother knight, one for whose country I have a fond regard, St. David, of Wales, in the gloomy castle of the Magician Ormandine, on the borders of Tartary. Go and free him. From trusting entirely to his own strength, and not seeking rightly for all other aids, he failed in what he undertook to accomplish. A magic sword, by which alone the Magician can be conquered, is held in a rock near his castle. No human strength can pull it out; but take this flask of oil, pour it into the rock, and, waiting patiently, you will find the sword easily come forth."

The Knight promised to obey the Fairy's directions; and she having disappeared, he and De Fistycuff set to work so manfully, although not accustomed to handle such tools, that in a few days they hewed themselves a subterranean passage beneath the walls of the city. Through iron plates, and thick walls, and granite rocks, and mud, and sand, they worked, the last, like slippery people, giving them the greatest difficulty to deal with. At length the sky appeared; and there, at the mouth of the cave out of which they emerged, stood their steeds, held by two dwarfs of ugly aspect, who presented them with their spears, and swords, and other weapons.

No sooner were they mounted, and St. George was about to reward the dwarfs, than he found that they had disappeared.

Accordingly, they set off, as fast as Bayard and the Squire's steed could carry them, along the neck of land which joins Africa to Asia, and then galloped rapidly northward. In wonderful condition were the horses, while the pure, fresh air their riders breathed, after their long imprisonment, added fresh vigour to their limbs, and courage to their hearts.

Many adventures, which cannot here be recorded, were met with; and at length they reached the magic forest which surrounded the castle of the fell Enchanter. They witnessed the same terrific sights, and heard the same sounds as did St. David and the faithful Owen; but, equally dauntless, they clove their onward way through brake and brier, in spite of the hissing of serpents and hooting of owls, groans and shrieks, and other similar sounds, to which they were pretty well accustomed by this time, till they reached the Magician's castle.

There, in the rock, they beheld the hilt of the magic sword. De Fistycuff was about to seize hold of it at once; but St. George warned him to desist till he wisely had obeyed the Fairy's directions, and poured the oil upon the rock. Slowly it trickled down through many a crevice, when the Knight, waiting patiently for the oil to take effect, grasped the sword with his left hand, while he kept his own falchion ready to use in the right.

"Who knows but the Magician may come forth to attack me before I have freed the sword?" he observed to his Squire. Gradually, but surely, the sword yielded to his unwearied and long-sustained efforts. While still drawing it forth, a terrific uproar was heard within the castle; the ground shook, trembled violently, rocking to and fro, and flames darted forth from the rock; but the Knight held fast the weapon.

Suddenly the brazen gates of the castle burst open, and there issued forth the Necromancer Ormandine, arrayed in all the terrors with which he could clothe himself. His helmet had a fiery plume, hissing snakes were writhing about his casque and shoulders, his armour seemed of red hot metal.

A hooting owl of hideous aspect sat on his shoulder, while he brandished an iron club covered with spikes, like his armour, red hot. He made directly at St. George ; but Ascalon was in the Knight's grasp, and wielding it, as he well knew how, he kept the Magician at bay, while he tugged more vehemently than ever at the magic sword.

With a clap louder than that of any thunder, it came at length forth from the rock, and taking it in his right hand he with it furiously assailed the Magician, who no sooner felt its keen edge than his club fell from his nerveless grasp, the owl flew hooting away, the serpents crawled hissing off, and the once-powerful Magician fell humbly on his knees and craved for mercy.

St. George, telling De Fistycuff to guard him, entered the castle, where, on iron beds, he found, bound with chains, his friend and comrade St. David, and the faithful Owen, groaning, and sighing, and mourning their hard fate. Cutting the chains, with as much ease as if they had been cords of silk, with the magic sword, he set them, to their great joy, on their legs, when, with a profusion of words, they poured out their expressions of gratitude.

St. David then told St. George of his vow to the Emperor of Tartary; when the English Knight informed him that the Enchanter was in his power, but that he was unwilling to take his life.

" But, behold the signs of his cruelty ! " said St. David, pointing out to St. George the other nine hundred and ninety-eight iron beds in the hall. " There lie bound many other noble knights and squires who for many long years have been prevented from engaging in any deeds of heroism.

Think how many victories they might have won;
how many captive knights released; how many
forlorn maidens rescued from durance vile; how
many other noble deeds they might have done!"

This speech so completely changed St. George's
view of things, that he told St. David he would
hand over the Magician to him. Then the Champion of Wales went forth from the castle, and with
one blow of his sword cut off Ormandine's hideous
head, and sticking it on a pole, which he delivered
to the faithful Owen to carry, informed his brother
Champion that he was ready forthwith to depart for
the court of the Emperor of Tartary.

The other nine hundred and ninety-eight gallant
knights and squires, released by the courage and
wisdom of St. George, having expressed a strong
desire to follow his fortunes, he undertook to lead
them round the world in search of adventures worthy
of their prowess. St. David, also, promised, when
he had fulfilled his vow to the Emperor of Tartary,
to search him out and aid him.

Often had the noble Champion of England
thought of the lovely Sabra, but knew not where
she was. At length, with his army of valiant
knights and trusty squires, having reached the kingdom of Bagabornabou, he, on inquiring for her,
heard, with dismay, that she had been carried off a
prisoner by Almidor, the black King of Morocco,
and had ever since been pining in a dungeon.

Calling his knights around him, he told them of
the occurrence, and with loud shouts, waving on
high their swords, they promised to accompany him
to rescue her, or to die in the attempt. Setting off
forthwith, they reached the dominions of the black

King; when St. George, disguising himself as a humble palmer, entered the city, followed by De Fistycuff, in the same habit, to ascertain in what vile dungeon the lovely Sabra was shut up.

In vain he wandered up and down, whispering her name, and inquiring of all he met, till, at length, he saw a beautiful white dove fly upward from a hole in the ground beneath the massive wall of a huge castle. Catching the dove, he wrote on a slip of parchment, which he placed under its wing, " St. George of England has come to Sabra's rescue. Tell me if you are here ! "

Soon the dove, having entered the hole, returned to the Knight, when he discovered, under its wing, on the same parchment : " I, the hapless Sabra, am here ; oh, free me, and receive a maiden's grateful love ! " Instantly returning to his knights, and throwing off his palmer garments, St. George led them to the assault.

On every side the castle walls were stormed. Some climbed up ladders, some over each other's backs, with such desperate valour, that the Moorish soldiers gave way on every side ; till Almidor, hearing the turmoil and loud shouts of war, rushed to the battlements. Then ensued a fight most desperate between the noble Champion of England and the black King, in which the latter would most assuredly have been slain had he not, like a recreant, turned his back and fled, among his followers, through a postern gate, which, happily for him, stood open,—proudly asserting that he would return and fight another day.

Having thus victoriously taken possession of the Moorish castle, St. George and all his knights and squires burst open all the doors and gates, and explored all the passages they could find, till they arrived at a gloomy vault. Within it was a little door. St. George thundered at it with his battle-axe. It burst open; and there he beheld his lovely and beloved Sabra, her beauty dimmed, but not extinguished, by her long imprisonment.

St. George and his knights having taken posses-sion of the Moorish capital, he held a grand banquet in honour of the occasion, when a herald announced, in due form, that the British Champion was about to wed the lovely African Princess. Thrice was the announcement made; and no one objecting, the fair Sabra, after all her misfortune, became, as her reward, the bride of the noblest Knight Europe, or the world, has ever known.

So enchanted were the Moors with the valour and courtesy of St. George, that their chiefs, lords, and nobles, and the councillors of state, came in humble guise and proffered him the crown of their country; but he declared, with many expressions suitable to the occasion, that he had not yet won that renown for which his soul panted, and must decline the honour.

Having dismissed the nine hundred and ninety-eight knights and squires, whom he had rescued from the castle of Ormandine, with warm thanks for the assistance they had rendered him, and sincere wishes for their welfare, they all departed to their separate countries and homes, and such as were married to their wives and children, who had long been mourning their absence, and in most cases, though not in all, wishing for their return; St. George and his beautiful bride, the enchanting

Sabra, set out on their travels, through many unknown and strange lands, attended by the faithful De Fistycuff, whose wife would much rather that he had gone back to look after her and their children in England.

CHAPTER XII

Now it happened that the great Emperor of the East held a grand tournament at Constantinople, to which all the knights and nobles of Christendom were invited, to do honour to his nuptials with a princess he was about to wed. Thither came the Seven Champions, not knowing each other after their long separation, but each believing the others in some distant quarter of the globe. The Emperor had, however, pitched seven tents of seven different colours, wherein the Seven Champions might remain till the sound of the silver trumpets summoned them to appear. Seven days the tournament was to last, and each day a different Knight was to be Champion of the field.

The first day, St. Denis of France, under the title of the Golden Knight, was the Champion. His tent was of the colour of the celandine, and on the summit flamed a sun of wondrous brilliancy. His horse, an iron grey, was graced with a plume of gold-bespangled feathers. Before him rode the faithful Le Crapeau, bearing his banner, on which was designed the golden *fleur-de-lis*. Numberless were the foreign knights with whom he tilted, every one of whom he overthrew

Next day, St. James of Spain, habited in silver

armour, rode forth as the Champion; his Squire, the faithful Pedrillo, bearing aloft four banners, on each of which were inscribed his names and titles, and those of his ancestors, so that not a spot of silk remained uncovered. Well he behaved himself, to the admiration of all beholders.

Clad in blue steel, and called the Azure Knight, on the third day, St. Anthony of Italy rode forth as the chief Champion, attended by the faithful Niccolo, bearing his standard, an eagle on a field of blue. Above his tent was a smaller pavilion in the shape of a watch-tower, in which was seated, as spectatress of the fights, the Georgian Princess, the strong-minded Rosalinde, who had, by praiseworthy perseverance, and allowing no trifles to stand in her way, completely won the heart of St. Anthony, and had become his bride. Well, also, did he, the Italian Champion, acquit himself, and many valiant knights were by his spear unhorsed.

On the fourth day, St. Andrew of Scotland was the chief Challenger for the tournament. His tent was framed in the manner of a ship swimming on the waves of the sea, environed about with dolphins, tritons, and many strangely-contrived mermaids; on the top stood a figure of Neptune, the god of the sea, bearing in his hand a streamer, whereon, in one corner, was wrought a cross in crimson silk. He was called the Red Knight, for a blood-red cloth completely covered his charger. His worthy achievements obtained such favour in the Emperor's eyes, that he threw him his silver gauntlet, which was prized at a thousand portagues, and the which Murdoch M'Alpine, lifting it from the ground, bore with no little satisfaction to his master's tent;

where the Champion also retired, and after his noble
encounters enjoyed a sweet repose.

The fifth day, St. Patrick of Ireland, as chief
Champion, entered the lists, mounted on an Irish
hobby, covered with a green veil. He was attended
by the faithful Terence O'Grady, in sylvan habit,
bearing on his shoulder a blooming tree, his motto,
virtus semper viret. His tent resembled a summer
bower, formed chiefly of the shamrock, and beauti-
fied with wreaths of roses. He was named the
Green Knight; but he was green only in name, for
no Knight proved himself more accomplished, or
performed nobler deeds.

Upon the sixth day, the famed Champion of
Wales entered the lists, mounted on a Tartar steed,
which was covered with a black cloth, to signify,
as Owen ap Rice made known, that a black and
tragical day was this for all Knights of every nation
who durst approve his fortitude. On his shield was
portrayed a silver griffin rampant, and upon a golden
helmet, the ancient arms of Britain. His tent was
in the form of a castle, the battlements guarded
by numerous sturdy men-at-arms. His princely
achievements not only obtained due commendations
at the Emperor's hands, but all the fair and high-
born dames present (so the faithful Owen ever
afterwards averred) applauded him as the most
noble Knight that ever shivered lance, and the most
fortunate Champion that ever appeared at the Court
of the Eastern Emperor.

Upon the seventh and last day, St. George of
England entered the lists as chief Challenger,
mounted on a sable-coloured steed, betrapped with
bars of burnished gold, and whose forehead was

beautiful with a gorgeous plume of purple feathers, from whence hung many pendants of gold. The Knight's armour was of the purest steel inlaid with silver; his helmet was richly adorned with pearls and many precious stones; and on his banner, borne before him by the faithful De Fistycuff, was pictured, on a blood-red field, a lion rampant, bearing three crowns upon his head. His tent, white as the feathers of the swan, was supported by figures of four elephants of purest brass. Before it stood an ivory chariot, guarded by twelve coal-black negroes, and in it sat his lovely bride, the Princess Sabra, spectatress of the tournament. All eyes turned towards the English Champion, to gaze and admire. His steed bore him right nobly, and never gave encounter to any knight but both man and horse were speedily hurled helpless to the ground. That day the tournament lasted from the sun's uprising till the evening star appeared, during which time he conquered five hundred of the hardiest knights of Asia, and shivered a thousand lances, to the admiration of all beholders.

The tournament being over, the Emperor sent to St. George's tent a golden tree with seven branches, to be divided equally among the seven foreign Champions. There they all assembled; and what was their astonishment, when they removed their casques, to discover that they were the long parted and ancient comrades! Warmly they grasped each other's hands, and talked and laughed right pleasantly. High revelry, also, did they hold that evening in St. George's tent, and told each other of their adventures, exploits, and achievements. Jovially they quaffed full golden beakers of rosy

wine, and many a jovial song they sang, and many
a tale they told. All inquired who the lady could
be who had been seen on the summit of St.
Anthony's tent; when he confessed that the
strong-minded Princess Rosalinde of Georgia had
won his heart and hand.

" She, then, is sister of the six lovely Princesses
I had the happiness of being instrumental in turning
from swans into young ladies. Your bride will be
glad to hear that they appeared none the worse for
their transformation ! " exclaimed St. Andrew.

" Ah ! you do not know, then, what happened
after you left the country, my cousin of Scotland ! "
cried St. Patrick. " Ha ! ha ! ha ! They all set
off to follow you, unknown to their father. I met
them in a wood with their six maidens, wandering
alone, and had the satisfaction of rescuing them
from the power of some unpleasant enemies, among
whom they had fallen. I thought they would have
found you out before now."

" No, indeed, I have escaped them hitherto,"
answered St. Andrew, rubbing his hands. " One
of them might have persuaded me to marry her, and
that would not at all have suited me. I intend to
remain a bachelor for many a year to come."

" I wonder you did not offer to marry one of
them, at least, my brave Irish friend," observed St.
Anthony ; " it would have been but in accordance
with the acknowledged gallantry of your countrymen. I, too, should have been glad to have hailed
you as a brother-in-law."

" Faith ! so I would have married one or all of
them, if it hadn't been from the difficulty of making
a selection, and hurting the feelings of the rest ; for

a more amiable collection of young ladies I never set eyes on ; so I gave them a little chariot I had got, drawn by a few alligators and hippopotami, and advised them to go quietly back to their father's court, instead of gadding about the world as they were then doing. Whether or not they took my advice I cannot say, for when they went north I turned my horse's head, and, with my faithful Squire, rode away south."

Many other similar adventures to these were told by the old comrades, of which there is no space to tell.

But if the Knights were merry, much more so were their Squires. Joyfully they discovered each other, and agreed to meet together in the tent of the faithful De Fistycuff. Right jovial was the meeting, and huge the amount of the viands they consumed, and innumerable the beakers of Samian and Falernian wine they quaffed. Merry the stories they told of their numberless adventures, and facetious the songs they sang. Each Squire boasted loudly of the deeds of his master, and of the country to which he belonged; but no one boasted louder than did the faithful Owen ap Rice, of St. David especially, and of his own loved country, Wales. Terence O'Grady was not much behind him in that respect; while Murdoch M'Alpine declared that St. Andrew was one of the best of masters, and that if Scotland was not the finest and the largest country in the world, it was, at all events, the one he loved the best, just because it was Scotland and his native land.

"Your hand, old comrade," exclaimed De Fistycuff, springing up, "that's the very reason

why I like merrie England. She has her faults,
I'll allow; but though I've wandered nearly all the
world around, there's no country in my mind to be
compared to her, and with all her faults I love her
still."

"Bah!" exclaimed Le Crapeau, "she is not
equal to *la belle* France, at all events."

"Inferior to Italy, without doubt. Look, what
noble people the ancient Romans were!" observed
Niccolo, swallowing a handful of macaroni.

"The idea of comparing a little island to a
magnificent territory like Spain!" cried Pedrillo.
"Why, we were civilized, and a province of Rome,
while the British were painted barbarians, unknown to all the rest of the world."

Thus they disputed, but all in good humour, and
many a joke was bartered on the subject. All
things terrestrial must come to an end, and so did,
at length, the Knights' banquet and the Squires'
jovial supper.

The next day, scarcely had the Champions arisen
from their downy couches, whereon they had rested
their weary limbs, after the fatigues of the numberless
combats in which they had been engaged, when it
was announced that six foreign Princesses, of great
beauty, had arrived in the capital, and had been
witnesses of the tournament, in disguise. Some said
they had come in one way, some in another; and
among other descriptions of the mode in which they
travelled, it was asserted that they came in a chariot,
drawn by twelve tame alligators and as many
hippopotami.

"The Georgian Princesses, a crown against a
baubee!" exclaimed St. Andrew, starting up from

H

his couch. "Murdoch, go and find out, with all speed, and if it is the case, get ready our steeds and baggage without delay, or one of these strong-minded young ladies will be insisting on accompanying me to my ancestral halls in bonnie Scotland."

"They've run their game to earth; there's no doubt about it," cried St. Patrick, who had been fond of sporting in his youth, when he heard the news. "They deserve our brushes for their pains; and one thing must be said in their favour, that they are very pretty young women, and not at all afflicted with the ordinary prejudices and bashfulness which stands in the way of so many young ladies in finding themselves comfortable establishments. What say you, Terence? Don't you think that I might go further and fare worse?"

"Ah! faith! noble Master, that you might, unless, mark me, you get back to old Ireland; and there it isn't much difficulty I'd have in finding many a score of sweet creatures, to whom, it's my belief, these Georgian Princesses couldn't hold a candle."

The mention of his fair countrywomen (of whom St. Patrick was a warm admirer, and who is not who knows them?) artfully thrown in by his Squire, turned the Knight from the intention he began to entertain of making one of the Princesses his bride.

When the Seven Champions met at breakfast, they talked the matter over with due gravity. They recollected that there were six ladies and only five bachelor knights, two only being benedicts.

"But suppose we five were to marry five of the Princesses, one still would be like puss in the corner —she must be left out," observed St. Andrew,

who was evidently the least inclined of any of the
party to wed, and had arranged to start away
directly after breakfast.

" Oh ! one must become a nun," observed St.
Patrick. " It's a mighty pleasant sort of life to
those who don't like work, and are fond of being
utterly useless."

Scarcely was the breakfast over than the
Champions were summoned into the presence of
the Emperor ; and there, seated around him, were
the six Princesses of Georgia, radiant in beauty,
and looking bewitching and killing in the extreme.

" Fair ladies, and right noble strong-minded
Princesses, here are the Seven Champions of
Christendom. It has come to our imperial knowledge that you have left the Court of my brother of
Georgia, your royal father, for the purpose of
wedding one, if not more, of these right valorous
Champions, for in that matter there seems to be
some little difficulty. Make your choice, therefore,
most strong-minded Princesses ; whom will you
wed ? For, from the observations I have made of
these Knights' gallantry, I can pledge my imperial
word that they will not refuse your moderate and
modest requests."

Now, the six Princesses, on hearing these words,
looked unutterable things, and a roseate hue rushed
into their lily-like cheeks ; but their eyes did not
wander up and down the hall among the Knights,
for, with a constancy worthy of all admiration and
imitation, they fixed them on St. Andrew.

" He is the Knight who changed us from swans
into maidens, he is the Knight, for love of whom
we left our father's home, and in search of whom

we wandered, all forlorn, the world up and down, and with him alone do any of us wish to wed."

"Well spoken, fair Princesses," observed the Emperor. "That much circumscribes the question, and decreases the difficulty. Which of you desires to wed with the gallant Christian Knight? For, remember, that only one wife can he have, whatever may be the custom in Asia."

St. Andrew, who had never feared mortal foe or foes, giants, wild beasts, or evil spirits, began at these words to tremble in his shoes, and to regret that he had not recommenced his travels by daybreak.

The strong-minded Princesses all sat looking at him.

"I'm the one to marry him," cried the eldest.

The Champion's heart began to sink within him.

"I'm the one to marry him," cried the second.

"But I'm the one to marry him," cried the third.

"But I say that I'm the one to marry him," cried the fourth.

"But I declare that I'm the one to marry him," cried the fifth.

"You are all wrong!" exclaimed the sixth. "From the very first I am sure that it was understood clearly that I was to be his wife."

"Stay, sweet Princesses," observed the Emperor, calmly, "I see clearly that there has been some slight misunderstanding among you about this matter, and I am sure St. Andrew is too gallant a Knight to desire to make any five of you unhappy, or jealous' of the sixth. I, therefore, purpose to send you all back, under a proper escort, to your father's court, and I hope that you will there speedily find six noble knights to lead you to the altar of Hymen."

The six strong-minded Princesses made very long faces at the decision of the Emperor; but, as his decisions were always final, they could make no reply; though, when they once more turned their eyes towards the Scottish Knight, the spectators could not but remark that their expression was very much changed, and St. Andrew evidently thought it wise to keep at a respectful distance from their fingers.

" Certes, Master," whispered Murdoch to St. Andrew, " you are, to my belief, very well out of it."

" It's a mighty easy way of settling the matter," said Terence O'Grady, " but I wonder what the six serving maids are to do ! "

History reports, however, that they went back to Georgia, married six stalwart knights, and lived very happily afterwards, as did their six fair attendants, who, in like manner, married six faithful squires, who all in time became knights and great lords of the realm.

After the tournament and all the festivities were over, the Seven Champions prepared to depart, each for his own country; but, ere they commenced their journey, news arrived that all the great Pagan Powers had banded together to overthrow the Christian Emperor of the East, who, therefore, sent to entreat all the aid they and their followers could afford. With one accord they promised to raise an army, and to hurry back to his assistance.

St. George, leaving his youthful bride, the lovely Princess Sabra, in his castle near Coventry, soon levied a powerful army; and, setting sail, no longer as a knight-errant, but as a renowned general, he arrived with his forces on the coast of Portugal, where he was joined by the other six Champions, who each brought troops in proportion to the size of his country. So enchanted were the Portuguese with St. George, that, having no Champion of their own, they entreated him to become theirs, and have ever since retained him among their most honoured saints and heroes. Here St. George was chosen generalissimo of all the Christian forces, and, once more setting sail, he entered the Mediterranean. Then, landing on the coast of Morocco, he bethought him of punishing Almidor, the black King of that country, who was about to join the Pagan armies.

The Moors in vain endeavoured to prevent the landing of the Christian Champions. The battle was hot and furious. Almidor rushed to the van, where quickly he was singled out by St. George. Terrific was the combat, and never before was the Moorish Monarch so hotly pressed.

Now he had prepared, in full expectation of victory, a vast cauldron of boiling metal, in which he purposed, with fell intent, to cast the Christian Champions and their followers ; but when at length, unable any longer to withstand the far-famed sword of St. George, he fled in despair, to cast himself headlong in, and his example being followed by his generals and chief officers, the furious battle was brought to a speedy end, and the Princess Sabra was well avenged for the cruelties the black Almidor had inflicted on her.

Scarcely had this satisfactory event been brought about than St. George received the unwelcome news that the Earl of Coventry was besieging his castle in England, for the purpose of carrying off the

Lady Sabra, his bride, and now the mother of three blooming boys,—the wicked Earl having spread a report that the great Champion of England, whom no other foe could conquer, had yielded to the inevitable hand of death.

The brave Knight hastened back with the speed of lightning, when sad was the sight which met his eyes. His castle was burnt to the ground, and his lady had been carried off by the wicked Earl, and, as she had refused all his offers of marriage, had been accused of witchcraft, and lay in prison, condemned to be burned alive. What had become of his three blooming boys he could not tell.

Putting spurs to his horse, the Knight and De Fistycuff galloped into Coventry. There he met the Earl going out hunting; and there, in mortal combat, he laid him low.

Scarcely had the Earl breathed his last, acknowledging with his dying breath the lady's innocence, than the Princess Sabra was led forth to execution. Quickly her guards were put to flight, and mounting her on his horse, he bore her off to a neighbouring forest, where he might defy pursuit.

There, as they wandered up and down, one day they espied three beauteous boys, sleeping on a bed of roses, beneath a shady bower. The parents' hearts told them that the children were their own. They flew towards them, when they saw, seated at the further end of the bower a beautiful lady. Instantly St. George knew her as the kind Fairy who so often before befriended him, and who had now saved his children from the burning castle. Again and again he thanked the Fairy, who, smiling sweetly, vanished from his sight.

Leaving his children under the care of those wise tutors, named Industry, Attention, and Teachableness, taking his wife, he once more set out to rejoin the army engaged in the war with the Pagans.

CHAPTER XIII

ST. GEORGE and his virtuous Lady, having arrived in Africa, were travelling to Egypt from the west, when they chanced to arrive at a magnificent country, inhabited only by Amazonians.

Journeying along, great was their surprise to find every town and village desolate of people ; the fields untilled ; and fields overgrown with weeds : nor man, nor woman, nor child was to be seen. Scarcely food even from the berries in the woods could they procure to satisfy their hunger.

In this extremity, after many days, they arrived before a rich pavilion—all of green and crimson, bordered with gold and azure—the hooks of ivory, the cords of silk, while at the top stood a golden eagle, and at each corner a green silver griffin shining in the sun. Beautiful as was the tent, still more lovely was the lady who stood before it—a maiden queen—crowned with an imperial diadem, and clothed in a robe of green, with the body formed of lace of gold, and her crimson kirtle bound with violet-coloured velvet, the wide sleeves being embroidered with flowers of gold and rich pearls. Around her stood her maiden attendants in comely attire, with silver coronets on their heads, and silver bows in their hands, while at their backs hung quivers full of golden arrows.

With courteous words the Queen invited the Knight and his Lady to enter her pavilion, when she told him that her country was sorely afflicted by the arts of a wicked magician, named Osmond, who had sought her love, and having been rejected had conceived the most deadly hatred against her.

"He has built," she said, "a mighty tower on the borders of my realm, from which issues so deadly and dark a smoke that my people are driven from their homes, and the country remains desolate. He has left the guarding of the castle to a terrible giant, the ugliest monster eyes ever beheld. He is thirty feet in height, his head three times the size of that of the largest ox, his eyes larger than two sunflowers, and his teeth, with which he can break a bar of iron, standing out a foot from his mouth; his arms long and bony, his skin black as coal and hard as brass, and his strength so great that he can carry away three knights in armour, and their steeds, with the greatest ease."

"Now, by my halidom, but I will fetter this monster and break the enchantment, or never see this place again." In vain the Princess Sabra entreated him not to undertake the adventure. Even the Amazonian Queen thought it beyond his power.

At daybreak, accompanied by De Fistycuff, he set forth, leaving the side of his weeping wife, and assuring her that he would return in safety. As he and his Squire advanced into the enchanted district the light of day decreased ; darker and darker it grew, till they could with difficulty grope their way before them, while dense clouds of smoke seemed to be rolling thicker and thicker over their heads.

Nothing could surpass the melancholy and depressing gloom of the air.

At length, by a faint glimmer of lurid light, they beheld the gates of the enchanted tower, at which sat, on a block of rock, a huge giant in his iron coat, with a mace of steel in his hand. At first sight of St. George and his Squire, he beat his teeth so mightily together that they rang like the stroke of an anvil; and then he sprang up and rushed forward, thinking to take the Champion, horse and all, within his mouth, with the Squire under one arm, and to bear them into the tower.

When, however, the giant opened his mouth, showing his teeth sharp as steel, St. George thrust his trusty sword Ascalon so far down it, that the monster cried out loud as thunder in his pain and terror; the very earth trembled, his mouth smoked like a fiery furnace, and his eyes rolled in his head like brands of flaming fire: but the Champion pressed him harder and harder, the blood flowing in a great stream from his mouth, till he was forced to cry out for mercy, and to beg for life. This St. George granted him, on condition that he would discover all the secrets of the tower, and ever after be his true servant. Then the giant swore to speak the truth, and told him that the necromancer had made a huge fire in a deep vault whence all the smoke came forth, but that near the fire was a fair and pleasant fountain, the water of which, if any knight could cast it on the fire, the smoke would cease and the fire be put out. This sufficed St. George.

Ordering the giant to keep the door, and leaving De Fistycuff to watch over him, he advanced into

the tower, which was full of vast windows; and
then he entered a long dark passage with a door at
one end, set as thick with spikes of steel as are the
prickles of a sea-urchin's skin; yet, dashing open
the door, in spite of the clouds of smoke which
rushed out, he descended in total darkness,
thundering blows all the time raining down on his
burgonet, which he guarded off with his shield, and
voices from unseen spirits screeching in his ears,
while the heat, great at first, increased so fiercely
that he was almost melted, his armour becoming
nearly red hot.

Just as he was about to faint he espied the
crystal fountain, and quickly filling his shield from
it, he cast the water on the fire.   Backwards and
forwards he went, till, to his joy, he saw the smoke
ceasing and the blue sky appearing, when the light
of the sun entering the dark passage, he saw on the
stairs many great images of brass, with mighty maces
of steel, which had struck him the heavy blows as
he descended.

The fire being quenched, and the enchantment
being thus happily quashed, the country was
restored to its former prosperous condition, while
St. George received warm thanks of the Amazonian
Queen; and then, with the Princess Sabra by his
side, and followed by De Fistycuff, and the huge
Giant Orcus as he was called, he set off to join the
Christian army in the south.   On their way, however, finding that they were not far from Bagabornabou, the native land of the lovely Sabra, they
determined to journey thither.

De Fistycuff, as a herald, went before to
announce their arrival, whereon they were received

right royally. Such joyful sounds of bells, trumpets, cymbals, and drums, were scarce ever heard
before in the kingdom; nor had such stately
pageants ever been seen as those which welcomed
them; the walls were hung with Indian coverlets
and curious tapestry, and the pavement was strewed
with odoriferous flowers of every lovely hue.

This being over, the Princess Sabra was crowned
Queen of the country, and for many days she and
her noble lord reigned there in peace and prosperity,
till the desire of martial glory summoned St. George
once more to buckle on his armour, and to join the
Christian forces now marching towards Egypt.

Time will not allow a full description of the
bloody battle which took place between the
Christians and the Pagans, or of the magic arts
practised by the fell Enchanter Osmond, who
strove with all his power to overthrow or circumvent the former; or how he raised an army
of evil spirits from the earth, the air, and fire, and
water; and besides a mighty tempest by which
huge oaks were torn up by the roots, houses and
temples were unroofed, and men and horses carried
high up into the air, and let down again with terrific
crashes.

While the tempest was raging, they charged into
the Christian host with flaming falchions, firing their
horses' manes, burning their trappings, and consum-
ing their banners; but undaunted they stood, headed
by St. George and the six other Champions, till the
Pagan forces were compelled at length to give way,
and to retire from the field.

The acts of the Enchanter were not yet concluded, for he erected a magic tent, with arts so

subtle, that the interior seemed like a large country full of gardens, fields, and orchards, and palaces. There he caused six of his spirits to assume the guise of six lovely princesses, travelling the country round in search of six gallant knights who would break some lances in their services. By artful guile the seeming royal ladies persuaded the six Champions to accompany them to their pavilion, where they announced that a right royal banquet was prepared to do them honour.

The Champions departed, unsuspicious of ill; but day after day passed by and they did not return. The troops, by degrees, began to complain that they were left without their leaders; when St. George, inquiring into the matter, right wisely supposed that it might be some cunning device of the Enchanter Osmond.

On inquiring of his slave, the Giant Orcus, he found that this was indeed too true, and that the Knights were kept in servile bonds in the magic pavilion. Addressing his warriors, he told them of the discovery he had made, when, with loud shouts, they vowed to follow wherever he might lead.

Thus trusting in the noble Champion, they neither feared the necromancer's charms, the flaming dragons, the fierce drakes, the flashing lurid lights, or the legions of hideous monsters armed with burning falchions, which surrounded them as they marched towards the enchanted pavilion. Far more dangerous were the sounds of sweet music which struck upon their ears, and the enchanting sights which their eyes beheld, as they surrounded the magic tent; but St. George, recollecting the honour of his knighthood, let drive at the tent with his sword, so furiously, that he cut it into a thousand pieces; when there was exposed to view the fell Enchanter Osmond, sitting on a rock of iron, feeding hideous spirits, who obeyed his will, with drops of blood.

The Champion and his soldiers rushed upon him so furiously that, seizing him unawares, they carried him off, and bound him with chains to the root of a blasted oak, whence neither his own art nor all the spirits he once commanded could release him.

St. George then set at liberty the six captive Knights, when the lovely princesses, turning into their proper shapes of six hideous spirits, flew off with loud shrieks and hisses through the air

The necromancer then shrieking forth that all his magic arts and devices had come to nought, tore out his eyes, bit his tongue in two, because that it had so often uttered curses, cut off his hands, which had held his silver wand, the cause of so much evil; and finally ended his existence by devouring his own inside, dying thus a warning to all magicians for future ages.

This adventure being happily terminated, the Christian army advanced towards Egypt and Persia; nor did the Champions ever again sheathe their swords, or unlock their armour, till the subversion of those ancient Empires was accomplished. This being done, they took truce of the world, and triumphantly marched towards Christendom; in which journey they erected many stately monuments in remembrance of their victories and heroical achievements; and through every country that they marched there flocked to them an innumerable company of Pagans, that desired to follow St.

George into Christendom, protesting that they wished to forsake their heathen gods, whose worshippers' chief delight is in the shedding of human blood and every cruelty. To their requests St. George at once condescended, not only in granting them their desires, but also in honouring them with the favour of his princely countenance.

Once more did the gallant Champion return to England, with the faithful De Fistycuff, and this time he invited the other six Champions to accompany him.

Pen would fail properly to describe the magnificent entertainments with which they were honoured, and the pleasant time they spent there, before they again set forward on their adventures.

There, sad to relate, the Princess Sabra sickened and died, and with grief and anguish St. George raised a magnificent tomb to her memory, and placed it above her grave. Then, after embracing his three young sons, he once more set out on his travels.

CHAPTER XIV

NUMBERLESS were the strange adventures in which the gallant Champions of Christendom were engaged, and numberless the noble deeds they performed; of the greater number of which this history, by stern necessity, must be silent, and many of which can be but briefly described.

For many years St. George had travelled up and down the world, the faithful De Fistycuff by his side, nor had news of them been received in England. His three noble sons had now grown to man's estate, and had received the honour of knighthood from their Sovereign. When, as they were visiting one night their mother's tomb, her spirit, in the gentle form she wore on earth, rose from out of it before their enravished eyes, and counselled them, as they loved their honoured father's memory, to go and search him out, and bring him back in safety to his native land. Thus having spoken, with a sweet smile, she vanished from their sight.

Well furnished, they set off from England. Scarcely had they travelled far through Normandy, than, as they were passing through a wood, a loud shriek assailed their ears. Charging amid the trees, they beheld a lovely damsel in the hands of a dozen armed men; fierce pirates, from their dress and weapons, they appeared. With the war-cry of their father's name, they rushed on the marauders, and, as none would yield, they slew them all, and then loosed the lady and her attendants, whom the pirates had bound to the surrounding trees.

With grateful words and tears, which chased each other down her cheeks of lily white, she told them that she was the daughter of a Duke, whose castle was hard by. Then the three young Knights were sumptuously entertained and pressed by the Duke to stay; but mindful of their duty, they speedily set forth again to search out their father.

They journeyed on for many days, through countries where no houses or habitations were to be found; they rested, therefore, at night in the woods or on the open downs, having only the starry firmament for their canopy. Thus sweetly reposing on their mother earth, they slept as soundly as if they had rested on beds of feathers, and had been surrounded with curtains of the purest Arabian silk.

One night they had been sleeping securely, until such time as Aurora began to gild the firmament with her bright rays, and to usher in Phœbus's golden light, when suddenly a terrific noise, which seemed to arise from some deep abyss, and to be about to rend the rocks asunder, assailed their ears.

Awaking, they leaped to their feet, and buckling on their armour, stood on their guard. High time it was for them so to do; had they slept but another minute sad would have been their fate. As they gazed around, to discover whence the noise could have proceeded, they saw coming towards them a most hideous monster, of excessive size and terrible shape. His eyes were like burning saucers, so round and large were they; his mouth was like that of some huge bird of prey, and his front claws were like those of eagles, but infinitely larger and sharper; he had ears like a fox, with a scaly breast, and wings like a bird; but his body was shaggy, and his hinder feet were like those of a lion.

Again and again he roared most terrifically, and as he moved along his head reached high up among the boughs of the tallest trees. Their three horses, as he drew near, snorted and stamped on the earth, rearing up with terror, and almost broke from the ropes which secured them, for the young knights, disdaining to fly as they might have done, had kept on foot. They felt, also, how perfectly and completely they could trust each other, and thus they stood, fearless of the coming danger.

The monster, with loud cries, spreading out his wings, and lifting up his terrible talons, rushed

towards them. Side by side, at a little distance
apart, they stood ready to receive him. He ran at
the centre one, who, stepping back a pace, made a
furious cut at him with his sword, while the other
two assailed him on either side. Quick as hail fell
their blows on his hard side, but, hard and tough
as was his skin, their sharp swords soon found
entrance, and the blood of the monster began to flow
in torrents, rising quickly over their feet, for they
fought in a valley from whence there was no means
for it to escape; blood not being able of itself to
run up hill in any way more easily than water, which
cannot do it at all. The young Knights thus saw
that if they desired to escape drowning, they must
finish the combat without further delay; the odour
of the monster was excessively disagreeable to their
olfactory nerves, being like the essence of ten
thousand pole-cats, weasels, skunks, ferrets, and
similar vermin.

Now they plied their blows more furiously than
ever, till at length Sir Guy, the eldest, plunged his
weapon into the monster's scaly breast, and roars of
pain and rage, louder than that which ten thousand
elephants, lions, and donkeys united could make,
were sent forth by the terrific brute, who threw
himself headlong on the gallant knights; but they
nimbly skipped out of the way; and, as his face lay
submerged in his own blood, they again thrust their
swords into his back and sides, while thousands of
bubbles, floating up from the surface of the pool of
blood, showed that, at length, he had breathed out
his hideous life.

The Knights, having ascertained that he was
dead, retired from the field; the neighbourhood of

which soon became unbearable, from the horrid odour which proceeded from it. Having thus washed away all the stains of the combat, in a neighbouring stream, for they were all three very nice young men, and hated to be more dirty than was necessary, they proceeded on their journey.

Time will not allow me to dwell long on their subsequent adventures.

As they journeyed on, faint and weary, and sadly wanting refreshment, they met a herald loudly proclaiming, on his brazen horn, the greatest rewards to whoever would slay the Monster Pongo, who was ravaging the country.

They stopped him and told him that they had slain the monster. On this, after they had shown him where the brute lay, the herald conducted them to the Court of the King, who received them with unbounded joy, and loaded them with honours.

Now it had happened, that, while the Monster Pongo was ravaging the country, and the King and all his Court, and ministers, and generals, and his army were distracted and entirely beside themselves, a band of pirates, led by a noted chief, had landed on their shores, and carried off the fair and young daughter of the King, the Princess Urania.

No sooner did the young Knights hear the tale, than they offered to go in search of her, as a work worthy of their arms. In a stout vessel, rowed by sturdy men, they set forth. Many tempests they met with, and much were they tossed about by the waves. Little did they think at the time that their honoured sire and his six friends, the other Champions of Christendom, were likewise making a long voyage, and were the sport of the winds and waves;

the only powers, indeed, which could make sport of such doughty Knights. Weeks had passed away, and still they were plowing the waves, and wishing that Britannia, when she was about it, had ruled them straighter, when they perceived, at a distance, several vessels.

They made towards them. A desperate combat was taking place, and fierce pirates, with burning torches in their hands, were endeavouring to set fire to the barks of their opponents.

On the deck of one of them, yet at a little distance, who should they behold but two of the great Champions of Christendom, their honoured father, St. George, and his dear friend, St. Andrew, standing calm and undismayed, waiting the time for their vessel to approach near enough to take part in the combat. As they guessed, rightly, the rest of the Champions lay on their couches below, overcome by the power of the sea, wishing themselves safe on dry land again, and caring very little whether they then and there went to the bottom.

Instantly the three young Knights, urging on their bark, threw themselves on the pirates, whom, after a desperate combat, they compelled to surrender; many having leaped overboard, and others having been slain. One of the pirate vessels was almost in a sinking state. A cry proceeded from her hold; it was that of a female in distress.

The young Knights rushed on board, when, ere the vessel sank, they drew forth a young and lovely damsel, and carried her in safety to their own bark. A few words sufficed to tell them that she was no other than the Princess Urania, of whom they were in search.

St. George was highly delighted with the prowess of his sons, and he and his friends accompanied them to the Court of Urania's father, where they were all, as might have been expected, sumptuously entertained.

From thence they again set forth in search of fresh adventures, which were no less wonderful than those I have already narrated, but which require a longer pen than mine to tell.

CHAPTER XV

TIME, which spares not kings or princes, any more than other people, at length laid his heavy hand on the Seven Great Champions of Christendom, and eke on their once doughty Squires. Hard knocks in battles and tournaments, voyages by sea, and travels by land, hard fare as well as gay revellings, fights with giants, monsters, wild beasts, and evil spirits, had done their work, unnerved their once iron arms, and turned their raven or auburn locks to grey; while from their chins, instead of full bushy beards, hung down long silvery streamers of white; and those lion voices, which once had been heard high above the din of battle, and had braved kings on their thrones and giants in their dens, were now changed to weak and trembling trebles, which could scarce be heard even above the summer breeze.

First, of St. Patrick I will tell. Laying aside his lance, and trusty sword, and armour, which he committed to the care of his ancient follower and faithful squire, Terence O'Grady, (now the father of a fine family, and settled on his own estate in

Ireland, which has been handed down to his descendants from generation to generation,) he assumed the humble palmer's guise, and resolved to wander up and down the world, not, as before, to perform feats of arms, but to collect all sorts of information which might be useful to his beloved native land, where he proposed ultimately to lay his bones.

No longer was he accompanied by his faithful Terence, but solitary and alone did the aged Palmer go forth. Great as he was, many sins had he to mourn, and much had he to be sorry for.

Among the things he most regretted were the opportunities he had lost of doing good, and of gaining that knowledge which would have made him useful in his generation. However, he thought that he would make amends for his early neglect; but even the great Saint had to learn that lost opportunities in the days of our youth and strength can seldom or never be recovered when years advance with rapid strides and lay a heavy hand upon us. Thus, resting on his staff, with a scallop shell in front of his broad-brimmed hat, in russet coat and wallet at his back, the old hero set out once more on his adventurous journey.

Many strange adventures even then befell him. Often was he assailed by fierce temptations, but bravely he resisted them, as he had done his enemies of old. The laws and institutions of foreign countries were the chief objects of his inquiries. Nothing came amiss to him; he asked about everything he saw, and never seemed weary of gaining information. Even into cook-shops and kitchens he found his way; and some assert that the Irish from him learned how to cook potatoes properly, though I do not see exactly how that can be the case, seeing, as may be remembered, that potatoes came from America, and that America did not happen to be known in those days. Perhaps he, however, may have been over there unknown to the rest of the world. Others say that, at all events, he introduced the Irish-stew; but to that there seems also some little objection of the same character, as "praties" enter largely into its composition.

Then, again, that objection is overruled by those who assert that some other root or some cereal might have been used in their stead. No true Irishman, however, doubts the following fact, which is about to be described.

Travelling onwards, he at length reached a part of Africa, often much infested by serpents. He was there told of a rare and wonderful means which the inhabitants employed to get rid of the serpents. Having caught them, they tied fish-hooks to their tails. No sooner did the serpents find this incumberance attached to them, than in their rage they never failed to turn round and bite at their other extremities. In this way they invariably caught their mouths in the hooks, and thus being turned into hoops or rings, from which uncomfortable position being utterly unable to escape, they were easily caught up on long sticks and thrown over the left shoulder into the nearest lake or river, from which they were certain never again to come back.

This was only one, it must be remembered, of the many important pieces of information that

blessed Saint and great man St. Patrick picked up
in his latter travels. Some say that he taught the
Irish to read and write. Certain, at all events, it is
that he introduced that fine and glorious weapon,
the shillelagh, among them ; and, moreover, taught
them the use of it, for which his memory is ever to
be held in due reverence, not to speak of many
other reasons why he should be loved and admired
by all the sons of Erin.

At length, St. Patrick, feeling that his latter days
were approaching, got back safe to Old Ireland,
there firmly purposed to leave his bones. The
country, at that time there can be no manner of
doubt about it, was overrun with serpents, big
and little, in great numbers, whose bite was so
venomous, that, if a man got stung by one of them,
he in a minute or less swelled up into a mountain.
So the people came to St. Patrick,—for to whom
else should they go, seeing that, of course, he was
one of the wisest men in the kingdom ?—and they
told him that it was their firm belief that the whole
land, from north to south, would be depopulated
before long if the snakes were not driven out of it.
So, just then thinking of something else, he told
them to take their shillelaghs and to knock the
snakes on the head, and to drive them into the sea,
he himself setting the example ; and right lustily
he laid about him, as he was wont to do in his
early days, among Pagan hosts, or wild beasts, or
giants, or ogres.

Suddenly, as he was attacking a monstrous
serpent wriggling about before him, he recollected
the way in which he had seen the snakes got rid of
in Africa. So, ordering all the fish-hooks to be

procured throughout Ireland to be brought to him, he had them tied on to the tails of all the serpents to be found. Instantly the serpents were turned into hoops, and calling his faithful followers, he showed them how to ring them all on their shillelaghs. This done, staggering away with them at their backs, all the serpents, and snakes, and vipers, were carried off to the sea, into which they were thrown and drowned, and from that day to this not one has ever ventured to come back to the shores of Old Ireland, and none ever will, that we may be assured.

After this great and important achievement, the pious Saint wished to retire altogether from public life. So he had a hermitage cut for himself out of a big grey moss overgrown rock, on an island in a lake surrounded by trees, where very few people ever thought of coming to see him ; but some good pious families, who lived near, used to take him fish, and other provisions, to supply his daily wants, which were, indeed, but few.

There he lived on for some years, his existence being neither very useful nor very interesting, and the puzzle was how he managed to pass his time. His hair grew longer than ever, and so did his nails ; and at length it was discovered that he was with them, day after day, engaged in digging his own grave. Like the mole, working away, he turned up the earth till he had made it deep enough and long enough to suit his taste. When it was completed he laid himself down in it, weary of the world, and never rose from it again.

When the peasants came the next morning, they found the old Saint dead ; so, mournfully they threw back the earth he had turned up; and many years afterwards, the exact spot being ascertained, a magnificent church was raised over it to his memory

CHAPTER XVI

PEN would fail to write, or man to tell, all the gallant achievements which the noble Knight, St. David of Wales, and his faithful Squire, Owen ap Rice, performed during their foreign travels.

At length even they began to weary of the constant hazardous adventures in which they were engaged. Age had begun to dim the lustre of St. David's eye, and to unnerve his arm, but not to lower the courage of his heart.

News was now brought him that an army of Pagan barbarians was about to attack his native land. No time was to be lost if he would render service to his country. On his homeward way he collected all the gallant knights, and their squires, and men-at-arms, with whom he and the faithful Owen had, in their travels, become acquainted. Thus, by the time he reached the borders of Wales, he had assembled an army which, though small, was well able to perform deeds such as ten times the number of ordinary men would not have dared to attempt.

Sad was the state of Wales when they entered it in battle-array, seeking the enemy,—towns were unpeopled, houses overthrown, monasteries pillaged, corn-fields burnt, farms destroyed, while from the caves and woods came forth the unhappy people, to welcome him as their deliverer, and to pray for his success.

These sights so fired the spirit of the aged Champion, that he vowed never to rest till he had driven the enemy from his native soil. Still the task was no easy one. They were very numerous, fierce, and brave, and trained to arms.

The aged bards of Wales struck their harps to encourage the warriors to strive bravely in the fight.

It was, however, discovered that many recreant knights had joined the forces of the Pagans; they and their followers being habited in armour little differing from that of the Champion of Wales and those knights who had accompanied him from abroad.

Summoning his warriors around him, he addressed them in a speech which encouraged and animated their valour to the highest pitch. Thus he concluded : —

" Then follow me, my gallant warriors ! I will give the signal for the onset, which will lay thousands of our foemen low ; and see, for my ensign, I do wear upon my burgonet this leek, which will, if we gain the victory, be ever after held in honour throughout Wales, and on this first day of March be worn by all Welshmen in commemoration of our victory."

Thrice struck the bards their harps, while cheers, loud and long, replied to the speech, each warrior of Wales forthwith plucking up a great leek, and placing it on his casque, or headpiece, so that in the thickest fight friends might be known from foes.

Now there stepped forth a bard, and struck a mournful strain.

> " Sad, sad are the notes I sing,
> And sad the news I bring,
> For many a gallant knight, and many a warrior bold,
> Will fall to-day,
> And turn to clay,
> Before swift time grows old.
> The noblest and the best before the eve must die,
> Ere the fell Pagan host are taught to turn and fly."

These words struck the gallant old Champion's ears. He had never at any time thought little of his own prowess, while he, like a true patriot, had always been ready to sacrifice himself for the good of his country. He resolved, accordingly, should the tide of battle set strong against his followers, to charge onward amid the hosts of the enemy, and to fall nobly among them, knowing that his friends, for the love they bore him, would, for the sake of recovering his body, charge into the midst of the foe, and assuredly retrieve the fortunes of the day.

With a cheerful voice, as if he had been giving orders for the commencement of a tournament, the noble old Champion gave the promised signal for the onset. Furiously charged the army of Welshmen. Bravely were they met by their Pagan foes, who, with valour worthy of a better cause, charged in return, and many on both sides sunk on the ensanguined plain never to rise again.

Knight after knight sank down under the terrific

blows of the Pagan clubs and battle-axes, till there seemed but little prospect that the patriot army would gain the victory. In vain the Christian army shouted and charged. The sturdy Pagans refused to give way.

At length, St. David, recollecting the words uttered by the prophetic bard in the morning, assembled round him his bravest knights, and, throwing up his visor, exhibited his countenance, whereon sat a beaming smile, expressive of patriotism and valour.

" One of the noblest in the land, it is said, must this day fall before the battle is won ! " he exclaimed. " If such I am, then happy shall I be to be thus honoured in my death. Charge ! brave knights, charge ! "

With these words, the last he ever uttered, the noble Champion rushed into the thickest of the fight, where a hundred battle-axes rattled on his helmet, a hundred swords were pointed at his side, a hundred spears thrust against his fearless breast, and a hundred arrows shot at his head. Pierced by a hundred wounds he fell, but his followers bravely avenged his death. The Pagan hordes were put to flight ; and St. David has ever since, even to the present day, been held in affectionate remembrance, as he fully deserved, by all Welshmen.

CHAPTER XVII

St. Denis of France, like his brother Champions, much desired, after his long wanderings, to see once more the smiling fields of *la belle* France, and thus he, too, followed by the faithful Le Crapeau, turned his steps homeward. Time had not failed to leave its hoary marks on him, and his snowy locks and flowing beard showed full well that the winter of his life had at length overtaken him. Still he kept his armour on, though his shrunken form often seemed to rattle within it ; and the chill blasts, as they entered the crevices, blew round and round him, and made him often wish for his arm-chair, and dressing-gown, and slippers, as does many another elderly gentleman, who would be far wiser if he kept by his own fireside, instead of allowing himself to be dragged about the world, in search of a very doubtful sort of advantage or amusement for the younger branches of his family.

St. Denis had not neglected in his travels to discover many things which he thought might be with advantage introduced into his native country. He taught the people how to cultivate the vine, and make *chaussé* roads, though the latter were never very satisfactory. But many cunning arts and manufactures also he introduced from the far east, of which there is not space now to speak. The greatest benefit, however, he conferred on his countrymen was in instructing them in the impor-tant art of cookery. Fricassees and ragouts were by his means brought to great perfection, and, more than all, he instructed them how to dress frogs and snails, of which art they were before his time totally ignorant. Who could ever imagine that there was a time when Frenchmen knew nothing of that important part of the culinary art ? Till St. Denis, the hero of a hundred fights, aided by the faithful Le Crapeau, caught the frogs and cooked them, and, moreover, eat them, the ignorant Frenchmen could not believe that they were intended to be used as food.

But mark the ingratitude of a people—the fickleness of a crowd. The great St. Denis, who had fought so long, and upheld the name of France in so many strange lands, was accused by a recreant knight of heresy and of high treason, and of endeavouring to introduce bad and mischievous customs among the people.

Old as he was, although he had long laid aside his armour, the fire of his youth burned up within him, and he challenged his malignant accuser to mortal combat.

The Champion and the false knight met; but the latter, by the arts of a wicked enchanter, had come so prepared by talismans for the fight, that all the skill and courage of St. Denis could not overthrow him.

Again and again the aged Champion charged with all the agility and courage of a young man, and few would have supposed that he who sat within that iron mask, and wielded that heavy lance, had seen near eighty winters pass over his hoary head. Once more he charged—his lance was shivered, and he was borne helpless to the ground.

Then were the evil designs of his fell enemy victorious. He was condemned to death. No rescue came, and he was led, yet habited in his armour, to the block. With a courageous look he lay down his head; but scarcely had the axe of the cruel executioner fallen upon it, than a fearful tempest burst forth. The headsman, the recreant knight, and all who had assisted willingly at the execution, were struck to the ground, becoming black masses of cinder, by a flash of fearful lightning; and then the people learned and acknowledged that right and justice were on the Champion's side.

Monuments were built and churches erected to his memory, and he was ever after reverenced as the Patron Saint of France and of all Frenchmen.

CHAPTER XVIII

St. James, as long as his arm could wield a lance, continued his heroic combats with pagans and infidels of all sorts, magicians and necromancers, giants and ogres, wild beasts and evil spirits of every kind, sort, and description; but he, at length, too, finding his strength departing, and his hair growing grey, resolved to return home. One day, however, as he was about to put on his armour, to ride forth as usual, he discovered that he could scarcely lift it.

"The time has come, my faithful Pedrillo, when no longer as a steel-clad knight, but as a humble pilgrim, I must wander through the world," he remarked, sitting down again on the couch from which he had risen. "Go forth, my faithful Squire, and purchase me a palmer's habit, a hat of grey colour, and a broad scallop shell. Never more will I put on yonder coat of steel. I should but disgrace the name I have so long borne as one of the bravest knights of Christendom."

[Well would it be if other generals and admirals would take a hint from St. James, and, following his example, would retire, when their powers are failing them, from public life.]

With a sigh the faithful Pedrillo went forth, and procured, as he was directed, a palmer's habit for his master, and one for himself. Their armour being packed up and carried on their war-steeds, they now, as pilgrims, journeyed homewards; but all who met them knew full well what they had been, and even midnight robbers and outlaws respected them, and allowed them to pass unmolested.

Thus travelling on, they reached at length the wide plains of sunny Spain. There St. James resolved to build a chapel, and to devote himself to its service. He erected also a hermitage hard by, where he and his faithful Pedrillo, who would not quit him, took up their abode as hermits. Then the peasantry from far and near came to visit them. Much good advice St. James could give them, and many things he taught them, while numberless were the strange stories he could tell of the wonderful things he had seen and done in foreign lands.

In time, his chapel, from the gifts brought to it, became one of the richest in the land; and this so excited the envy and anger of the monks of a neighbouring convent, that they conspired together to accuse him of necromancy and other terrible crimes.

St. James boldly refuted the accusations, and offered, once more, to try his lance against any friar among them who was man enough to put on armour and meet him in single combat; but they all declined the honour, though they did not the less hurl their invectives against him, and seek opportunities for his destruction.

At length, he and some of his more pious fellow-worshippers were caught one day inside their chapel. The doors were closed upon them, and the wicked monks, hiring a band of Pagan mercenaries, had them all shot to death by poisoned arrows. In spite of the pain they suffered, the Saint and his companions continued singing their hymns to the last, while a bright silvery light burst forth in the chapel—(so says the ancient chronicler)—which continued burning glorious as ever; and when, at length, the chapel was opened, the body of St. James and the bodies of his companions were found to be perfectly embalmed. Then they were placed in marble tombs with silver lids; and, to the present day, St. James, by all real Spaniards, is held in the highest esteem and reverence.

CHAPTER XIX

ABOUT the same time that his brother knights ended their martial career, St. Anthony, with his faithful follower, Niccolo, likewise, for the same reason, resolved to turn his face homewards. Rome was the city of his birth, and to Rome he went.

Rome was a Christian city, but there were still many Pagans in the neighbourhood, and many of the shrines had as yet scarcely been accommodated to the new faith, so that the pious St. Anthony had considerable difficulty in distinguishing one from the other. This very much grieved his heart. Even when he went among the priests he could not always make out to which faith they belonged. They made him long harangues, and assured him that their great wish was to develope their ancient and time-honoured institutions into whatever form was likely to prove most popular.

St. Anthony, who was a simple-minded man, was sorely puzzled by all this; so, after vainly endeavouring to comprehend the state of things in the ancient capital of the world, he retired to a hermitage, where he lived for the remainder of his days; nor would he ever again enter Rome. Thus, in the fragrant odour of sanctity, he died at a green old age.

CHAPTER XX

St. George and St. Andrew were the last of all the Seven Champions who remained together, rivalling each other in gallant deeds of arms.

Where breathes the Scotchman who does not desire, when his life's work seems almost done, to return once more to scent the air of his own free heathery hills, to climb their rocky heights, and to wander around their fertile vales? Strongly did the desire to turn homeward seize the heart of Scotland's Champion. He, however, did not lay aside his spear and sword; but old as he was, still clad in his armour, bestriding his war-horse, and followed by the faithful Murdoch, he kept steadily travelling on, day by day, towards the north.

Thus should the true knight do. Life is a battle from the beginning to the end—as the brave St. Andrew well knew; and never should the armour, the shield, or sword, be laid aside till death strikes the knell which summons the warrior from the world.

Many were the adventures he and the faithful Murdoch met with on their journey. More than one giant was slain, numbers of unhappy people released from slavery, and many districts cleared of wild beasts, before the aged Knight and his faithful Squire reached the fair shores of Scotia.

The fame of their deeds had gone before them, and all the nobility of the realm, and a vast concourse of people, assembled to do them honour. It was a proud day for the aged St. Andrew, when, clothed in his well-worn suit of armour, with Murdoch M'Alpine of that ilk carrying his spear by his side, he rode through the streets of auld Reekie, with the shouts of the delighted populace sounding in his ears and singing his praises.

"Long live St. Andrew! Long live St. Andrew! Wherever the Scottish name is known there will we Scotchmen boast of our own St. Andrew—of the gallant deeds he has done—of the name and of the fame he has won!"

Such were the cries which from far and near saluted his ears.

A grand tournament was also given in St. Andrew's honour, at which the aged Knight sat as umpire, though he wisely refrained from running a tilt, much as his heart tempted him to put on armour for the occasion.

Soon after this, being assured that feats of arms were no longer suited to him, he resolved to instruct his countrymen in certain important branches of knowledge which he had acquired in his foreign travels. To prepare himself for this

new work he retired to a hermitage he had built
high up on the side of a mountain. Thither,
however, in a short time, resorted to him all the
youths of aspiring minds who desired to acquire
information, and to receive instruction from the
sage. Thus, in process of time, the rude hut
became a spot celebrated for learning and piety.

There, happily and usefully employed, the old
warrior spent many years of his declining life.
But, alas! what virtue, what piety, can enable a
man to escape from the snares of enemies and
detractors? Accused of witchcraft, and other mal-
practices, the aged Saint was brought before some
stern judges, who forthwith condemned him to
death. Scarcely, however, had his head been cut
off than his innocence was discovered, and a church
was raised to his memory; and he has ever since
been held in honourable recollection by all Scotchmen as the Champion of whom his country should
be proud—a knight *sans peur et sans reproche.*

Such, however, is the way of the world.

CHAPTER XXI

THE last Champion who appears in this wondrous,
strange, and eventful history, is the great St. George.
Towards the fair land of his birth, right merrie
England, he, too, when he found age creeping on
him, resolved to turn his steps. Still lance in
hand, and clad in steel, his brave lion heart yet
undaunted, with the faithful De Fistycuff by his
side, he at length homeward set his eyes. His
faithful chronicler relates numberless adventures he

met with, scarcely less marvellous than those he encountered in his youth. Many a hard blow he got, which he still was able to return with interest, ably seconded by De Fistycuff, though, it must be confessed, his Squire had grown somewhat obese and unwieldy.

At length, the chalky cliffs of Britain, which for twice twelve years the noble Champion had never seen, came in sight. Joyful to him was the prospect; more joyful still the towns and villages, the pleasant aspect of the fields, and the green waving woods, as he travelled on towards Coventry. There, with warm greetings, the inhabitants of high and low degree received him.

Sadness, however, he saw on the countenances of many; and this was owing, as the veracious chronicler, from whose erudite work this history is drawn, informs us, to "a doleful report—how, upon Dunmore Heath, there raged up and down an infectious dragon, that so annoyed the country that the inhabitants thereabouts could not pass by without great danger; how that fifteen knights of the kingdom had already lost their lives in adventuring to suppress the same."

St. George no sooner heard thereof, and what wrongs his country received by this infectious dragon, than he purposed to put the adventure to trial, and either to free the land from so great a danger, or to finish his days in the attempt. So, taking leave of all present, he rode forward with as noble a spirit as he did in Africa, when he combated the mighty green dragon.

So, coming to the middle of the plain, he there saw his dreadful enemy, crouching on the ground in a deep cave. The monster, by a strange instinct knowing that his death drew nigh, made such a hideous yelling, that it seemed as if the sky was bursting with thunder, and the earth rocking with an earthquake. Then, bounding forth from his den, and espying the aged Champion, he ran with a fury so great against him as if he would devour both knight and steed, armour and all, in a moment. But the brave St. George, knowing well how to deal with dragons, and all such-like monsters, quickly wheeled his horse out of his way, and with such force did the monster rush on that he drove his sting full three feet into the ground. Returning again, however, with furious rage, he made at the Knight, and would have carried both him and his charger to the ground, but that St. George, thrusting his spear at his throat, the monster, to avoid it, threw himself back, and fell happily over, with his back on the turf and his feet in the air, wriggling about all the time his long forked tail. Whereat the noble Champion taking advantage, leaped from his horse, and, throwing down his sword, seized him in his arms before he could rise, and pressed his huge body so tightly in his arms, and held him there, that he squeezed the very life out of him; but alas! the dragon's sting annoyed the good Knight in such sort, that the dragon being no sooner slain and weltering in his venomous gore, than St. George likewise took his death's wound by the deep strokes of the dragon's sting, which he received in divers parts of his body, and bled in such abundance that his strength began to enfeeble and grow weak: yet, retaining his true nobleness of mind, he valiantly returned victor to the city of

Coventry, where all the inhabitants stood without the gates to receive him in great royalty, and to give him the honour that belonged to so worthy a conqueror.

No sooner, alas! had the brave old Knight arrived before the city, and presented the people with the head of the dragon which had so long annoyed the country, which was borne before him by the trusty old De Fistycuff, than, what with the abundance of blood that issued from his deep wounds, and the long bleeding without stopping of the same, he sunk back into the arms of his faithful Squire, and, without a sigh, he yielded up his breath. Great was the moan that was made for him throughout the country, and all in the land, from the King to the shepherd, mourned him for the space of a month. The King also, in remembrance of him, ordained for ever after to be kept a solemn procession by all the princes and chief nobility of the country upon the twenty-third day of April, naming it St. George's Day; on which day the brave old Knight was most solemnly interred in the city where he was born. The King likewise decreed, by the consent of the whole kingdom, that the patron of the land should be named St. George our Christian Champion, in that he had fought so many battles to the honour of Christendom.

Thus ends the ancient, authentic, and most credible chronicle from which I have quoted.

There are many other documents extant, giving accounts of the exploits of St. George's three sons, and of the sons of some of the other Champions of Christendom; but as I do not consider that they emanated from sources so reliable and unexceptionable as those chronicles from which I have quoted, I have not thought it advisable to introduce them in the present veracious narrative.

THE END